George W. Ranck

Guide to Lexington, Kentucky

with notices historical and descriptive of places and objects of interest

George W. Ranck

Guide to Lexington, Kentucky
with notices historical and descriptive of places and objects of interest

ISBN/EAN: 9783337225186

Printed in Europe, USA, Canada, Australia, Japan

Cover: Foto ©Andreas Hilbeck / pixelio.de

More available books at **www.hansebooks.com**

GUIDE

TO

LEXINGTON

KENTUCKY,

With Notices Historical and Descriptive of Places and Objects of Interest,
and a Summary of the Advantages and Resources of
the City and Vicinity,

BY

G. W. RANCK,

AUTHOR OF HISTORY OF LEXINGTON, O'HARA AND HIS ELEGIES,
SKETCHES OF KENTUCKY HISTORY, ETC.

ILLUSTRATED.

LEXINGTON, KENTUCKY:
TRANSYLVANIA PRINTING AND PUBLISHING COMPANY.

≈LEXINGTON.≈

No American city of its age can more justly claim the attention of the tourist than Lexington. It is rich in historic associations, is a complete epitome of Old Kentucky life and manners, and is surrounded by all the attractions of a region which, for pastoral beauty and fertility, is unsurpassed upon the face of the globe. Almost in its suburbs is the site of Bryant's Station, so celebrated for the siege it sustained at the hands of the British and the Indians a hundred years ago; noted old Boonsborough, and the tragic battle field of Blue Licks are not far distant, and within half an hour's ride from the city stands the highest pier bridge in the world in the midst of the wild and magnificent scenery of that wonderfully picturesque river—the battlemented Kentucky.

Lexington, the seat of justice of Fayette County, and the social and commercial capital of the famous "Blue Grass Region," is situated in what Bancroft styles, "the unrivaled valley of Elkhorn creek," and is, by rail, ninety-four miles east of Louisville and eighty miles south of Cincinnati. Her population is about twenty thousand. The streets, which are laid off at right angles, are adorned with handsome business houses and private residences, and the splendid macadamized roads, which radiate from the city in every direction, lead the tourist to landscapes strikingly English in appearance, dotted with veritable "Old Kentucky Homes," and with extensive stock-breeding establishments, where herds of thoroughbred cattle graze, and from whence have gone forth most of the noted blood horses of America. The annual sales of horses and cattle held here are the most extensive of their kind in the world.

Lexington has ten newspapers, four of which are daily; twenty-two churches, and twenty-three educational institutions, including one university , a new State College, a Commercial College, three large female seminaries, and flourishing public and private schools. Her railroad facilities have lately been greatly increased, and the outlook of the city is exceedingly encouraging. Trade which has heretofore been heaviest in grain, groceries, dry goods, whisky, hemp and live stock is opening new channels and extending and taking on a far more enterprising phaze. Within a few months a Chamber of Commerce, telephones, street railroad, electric lights, and a free mail delivery, have gone into operation, new public buildings are to be erected, new factories are being established, and the demand for houses is unprecedented. Lexington is becoming more and more important as a railroad center, and her superior advantages in this respect will make her for the second time the capital of the State. Coal is abundant and cheap ; the neighboring counties teem with it, and with iron and lumber of the most valuable kinds, and the fat and fertile region surrounding her will feed a vast population. The inducements to make her a manufacturing city are plain and strong, and everything invites the capitalist to investment.

BUILDING STONE.

Lexington enjoys superior advantages in the quality, variety and supply of building stone, two kinds of which are worthy of special mention. One, which abounds almost in the suburbs of the city, is very fine magnesian limestone, resembling the famous Caen stone of Normandy. It is popularly known as "Kentucky Marble," and is the stone of which the Clay monument was built. The other is known as Superior Freestone, and is quarried at Farmer's Station, a short distance out on the line of the Chesapeake and Ohio Railroad, and is the material of which the new Court House and pavements on Main street are being constructed. It is of two colors, buff and a bluish gray, presents a handsome appearance, and is of uniform texture, even, true and smooth. It is said to have been in use more than fifty years without showing signs of disintegration.

AS A POPULAR RESORT.

Owing to her central location, splendid railroad facilities, historic attractions, and fine hotel accommodations, Lexington is by far the most popular place in Kentucky for the holding of conventions, re-unions, festivals, mass meetings, and gatherings of all kinds. The number and variety of the assemblages that convene in Lexington is remarkable and steadily increasing. The exceeding healthfulness of the city; its pure air; grateful temperature and fine society, have always made it a favorite summer resort for visitors from the extreme South who are mindful also of its blue grass bill of fare, for it is doubtful if there is another equal body of land in existence that produces so many of the luxuries and substantials of life as the region around Lexington. The city is destined to reap no small advantage from the stream of travelers, tourists, and strangers, which will grow larger and larger as her attractions become more widely known.

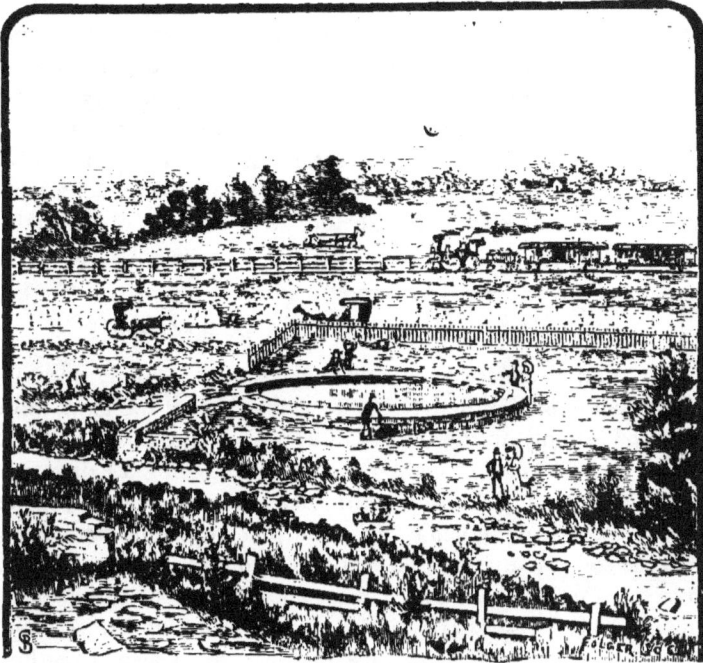

MULLEN.   PHOTO.

THE WILDERNESS SPRING.
(Where the City was Named.)

Tourists and visitors will be interested in the romantic, but perfectly authentic, incident which occurred at this spot, which is located at the west end of Pepper's distillery, on the old Frankfort road, in the suburbs of the city. The history of Lexington, which commences with the opening of the American Revolution, furnishes the anomalous instance of a city named four years before it was settled. About the fifth of June, 1775, at nightfall, a party of daring pioneers, headed by the celebrated Indian fighters, Robert Patterson and Simon Kenton, camped at what was afterwards called "Royal's Spring," which, after the lapse of more than a century, is as copious as ever. It is now encircled by a wall. Delighted with the prospect about them, they determined to make a "settlement" around the very spot where they were then encamped, and they named it "Lexington," as they excitedly discussed the thrilling news which had so slowly penetrated the depths of the dense wilderness of Kentucky of that momentous battle between "the Rebels" and "the Red Coats," which had been fought six weeks before in the

Colony of Massachusetts. This, then, was the first city named after that
historic field, and constitutes the first monument ever erected upon this continent to the first martyrs to the cause of American Independence, and as
such was toasted at Lexington, Mass.,on the 19th of April, 1875, at the great
centennial celebration of that battle.   The hunters who camped at the Wilderness Spring had barely named their future city when they were dispersed
by the savages, who, leagueing with the British, filled Kentucky with their
raging bands, and four years elapsed before the settlement of Lexington was
effected.

WHAT IS THE BLUE GRASS REGION?

Is a question strangers almost invariably ask. Strictly speaking the
Blue Grass Region of Kentucky is quite extensive, but the term, in its popular sense, applies only to the remarkable body of land in the center of the
State, which comprises six or eight counties surrounding Lexington. This
favored district, which a scientific authority has styled "the very heart of
the United States," is underlaid by a peculiar,decomposable limestone, which
imparts to the soil an unsurpassed fertility, and gives to our grass, known
to botanists as *Poa Pretensis*, a richness and permanent luxuriance which
it attains no where else.   Hence the term, "The Blue Grass Region," a
synonim for the acme of fertility of a district, which also bears the proud
distinction of "the garden spot of the world."   But why our rich grass is
called "blue" when it never is blue, is one of the unsolved problems.   It
is always green, except when in bloom, when the heads have a brownish-
purple tint.   If, however, the term "Blue Grass" is meant for an abbrevia-
tion of blue limestone grass, then it will do, for certainly it only reaches
it highest perfection on our wonderful blue limestone soil.   Propagated
without cultivation, it comes up thick and juicy early in the spring, ripens
in June, renews its growth in autumn, and, retaining its verdure in spite
of snow and ice,furnishes abundant and unequaled pasturage during the entire winter.   It is believed to be indiginous.

POPULATION AND MANUFACTURES.

It is stated on scientific authority that the State of Kentucky lies in the
center of the region now holding, and destined always to hold, the mass of
American population.   The location of Lexington in the very centre of
population makes it therefore practically certain that manufactures from
this city will always command *the widest markets with the least carriage.*

THE BLOCK HOUSE.

The site of this quaint old pioneer structure, which stood on the south-west corner of Main and Mill streets, will always be regarded with interest, as it is the place where the first permanent settlement of Lexington was made, and the scene of some of the most thrilling episodes of the days of the pioneers. In the spring of 1779 Colonel Robert Patterson, who had never forgotten the beautiful tract he had helped to name, set out from Harrods-burg with a little company of adventurers "to go up and possess the land,"

and about the beginning of April they erected the now noted block house. This lonely little outpost, which was watched by the Indians with unrelenting hatred, and which often sheltered the celebrated Daniel Boone, was conse-crated by suffering and blood, and its founder, Colonel Patterson, who was also the founder of Cincinnati and Dayton, figured in many of the most perilous and romantic incidents which adorn the annals of the "Dark and Bloody Ground." The spot upon which the block house stood is now occu-pied by the Carty Building.

HEALTH.

The healthfulness of Lexington may be inferred from the significant fact that the State of Kentucky has a mortality assigned to it by the statis-tics of the United States census as low as eleven per thousand, which seems almost incredibly small, but is borne out by the facts.

LEXINGTON'S WATER SUPPLY.

The water resources of Lexington are inexhaustible, and the abundance of its natural supply is one of the most remarkable features of the place, The city rests upon extensive strata of cavernous limestone, which abound with underground lakes and streams, which are easily tapped. A number of wells connect with these subterranean supplies. One of them (of soft water), on the McMurtry lot, and sixty feet deep, was provided with a large steam pump, which was in constant operation eighteen hours per day for many years, without perceptably reducing the supply. Another at the Lunatic Asylum was sunk about a hundred feet, when the augur dropped into a cavity and the water rose fifty feet in the bore. Two wells at the ice factory here supply water enough to run two engines and make twenty or thirty tons of ice per day, and the wells used by the railroad companies easily provide water sufficient for all the engines used to draw the fifty or sixty passenger and freight trains that daily arrive and depart at this place. The multitude of large and copious springs in and about the city still further indicate the extent of our subterranean water resources. It is from springs that all our extensive distilleries get their water supply, each of them using 200,000 gallons daily, to say nothing of the amount used by malt houses, dairies and other industries. The capacity of some of these springs is wonderful. The stream from Russell Cave Spring has sufficient volume to turn a mill. · The water that flows from Davis Bottom Spring and its connecting springs is simply enormous, and the depth of the noted Wilson Spring, near the city, is so great that it has been called the "bottomless spring." It is claimed that the united capacity of Wilson's spring and the two known as "Aters" is great enough to furnish eighty-seven gallons of water a day to each of twenty thousand persons by the natural flow of the water and without the use of a dam. Others assert that an abundant supply of water, capable of indefinite augmentation, could be obtained close to the city by suitably collecting and storing the waters of Wolf's Run, its neighboring streams, the numerous and copious springs, including Wilson's, that feed them, and the immense amount of surface water supplied by winter rains and melting snows, that could be gathered by excellent natural drainage in the extensive area which embraces these springs and streams.

There are still others who claim that the water supply that can be obtained through surface drainage on the Wickliffe farm, in the suburbs of Lexington. would be ample for the whole city. It is evident from these facts that the water resources of Lexington are various, and inexhaustible and capable of a development to meet all the demands of mills, manufactories and progress.

THE CARTY BUILDING.

(Site of the Block House.)

On the southwest corner of Main and Mill streets attracts the attention of visitors and strangers, as the site of the famous block house where the settlement of Lexington commenced, and as the seat of the Commercial College of Kentucky University and of the Young Men's Christian Asso-

MULLEN.   PHOTO.

ciation. The flourishing Commercial College with its two large halls corps of teachers, and crowds of pupils, furnishes one of the most animated sights of the city. Over three hundred young men from twenty-two States have graduated from this College in eleven months. It claims the largest attendance of any institution of its kind in the West or South; is the only Business College connected with a chartered University of note and high standing and the only one whose halls are especially designated for instruc-

'tion in all departments of Business Education. E. W. Smith, Principal;
Wilbur R. Smith, President.

.   The Young Men's Christian Association which freely and cordially
invites visitors and strangers to share its benefits and hospitalities, occupies
a large and handsomely furnished hall on the second floor of this building.
It has a library, many newspapers on file, magazines, and popular periodi-
cals, and is a "live" institution. President, R. S. Bullock; General Secretary, C. S. Ward; Maj. H. B. McClellan, W. R. Milward, R. H. Courtney,
A. J. Campbell, Wilbur R. Smith and others are also officially connected
with it.

The Schools of Telegraphy and Phonography, drug establishment of
H. H. Barnes & Co.; dental office of Dr. J. T. Hervey, and Cohen's clothing store are in this building.

THE OLD FORT,

(See Frontispiece)

Which comprised the whole of Lexington a hundred years ago, included
the block house and the cabins of the early settlers, which were gradually
connected with it as a defense against the Indians. The block house, which
had formerly stood alone, had become in 1782 only one angle of the fort
which rude, but powerful fortification, embraced a large part of Main street,
between Mill and Broadway, now covered by business houses. It was once
surrounded by Colonel Byrd and his swarming bands of savage allies ; was
the favorite retreat of General George Rogers Clarke, the "Napoleon of the
West;" and was the rendezvous of many a sudden expedition against the
murdering red-skins. Its garrison aided in the defense of Bryant's Station
when it was besieged by the Indians under the notorious Simon Girty ; en-
dured the horrors of the famous "winter of starvation," and shared in the terrible disaster of the Blue Licks, which left so many widows and orphans
within its walls. After this last-named massacre an Indian, who had skulked
behind the savage army to plunder the bodies of the slaughtered whites, was
killed by one of the Lexington garrison, and the settlers, burning with indig-
nation and wild with grief over their great calamity, mounted his head upon
a pole, which they planted upon the roof of the block house. It was from
this fort that Boone made one of his most remarkable rifle shots, killing an
Indian who, on the site of the present jail, was kneeling to scalp a settler he
had wounded. Tragedies, bloody afflictions and thrilling adventures were
of almost daily occurrence about the old fort, and the hardships and the suf-
ferings of the Puritans of Plymouth were fully equaled by the early settlers
of Lexington.

1

MORRISON COLLEGE.

This remarkable building, which stands in the extensive campus at the head of Mill and Market streets, rarely fails to attract the attention of the intelligent stranger, as it was for many years the seat of famous old Transylvania University, which acquired it through the liberality of Col. James Morrison, a wealthy citizen of Lexington, and a munificent patron of letters. Transylvania University was the first institution of learning established in the West, having been chartered by the Legislature of Virginia as

early as 1780, and General Washington, John Adams and Aaron Burr contributed to its endowment. It subsequently attained great prominence and influence. Its name was respected throughout America, and its celebrity extended to Europe. It was visited by President Monroe, General Jackson, Lafayette and Daniel Webster. Among those who filled its chairs may be mentioned Henry Clay, one of its law professors; Dr. Holly, its most brilliant President, Rafinesque, the eminent Scientist, and Dr. Ben. Dudley, the celebrated surgeon. The Confederate ex-President, Jefferson Davis, was a pupil of Transylvania, and in the long list of its distinguished graduates occur the names of William T Barry, Richard M. Johnson, John Rowan, Thomas F. Marshall and Richard H. Menifee. It was in the chapel of Morrison.

College that Henry Clay was admitted to the communion of the Episcopal Church, which was then temporarily occupying it. In 1865 Transylvania was merged in Kentucky University, which was founded by John B. Bowman, who was for many years its regent, and Morrison College is now the seat of that well known and ably-equipped institution. Kentucky University consists of four colleges; is under the auspices and control of the Christian Church, and is steadily progressing, with Dr. C. L. Loos as President. Rich in historic associations, in a splendid condition financially, and provided with a corps of first-class instructors, Kentucky University is an educational attraction destined to draw increasing numbers of young men to her classic halls, and no city in the Union welcomes earnest students more heartily than Lexington.

BRYANT'S STATION.

Celebrated as the place where, in 1782, occurred one of the most remarkable sieges recorded in the history of savage warfare, is about five miles northeast of Lexington, and is quickly reached by the Kentucky Central Railroad or by turnpike. Here a handful of pioneers, with desperate bravery and after many thrilling experiences, successfully defended the rude station of a hundred years ago against six hundred Indians under the able leadership of the notorious renegade, Simon Girty. The noted spring around which the savages concealed themselves, and where the heroic women of the garrison faced a horrible death to obtain the water that saved the fort, still pours forth a grateful stream. The site of the old station is unmistakable, and the graves of some of its defenders can still be seen.

GRATZ PARK,

A perfect little gem of a place for public recreation, established through the efforts of Mr. H. H. Gratz, of the Kentucky Gazette, is between Second and Third Streets, fronting Morrison College. It is classic ground, being the original site of Transylvania University; the home of its distinguished President, Dr. Holly; the place where Jefferson Davis played and studied as a school boy, and the scene of memorable events in which figured many of the noted characters of this country and of Europe. The old well in this park, from which Lafayette drank, was dug for the University about ninety years ago by John R. Shaw, the famous water wizard, and the most excentric and unfortunate character known to early Lexington. The Park was named in honor of our highly esteemed fellow-citizen, the venerable Benjamin Gratz, Esq.

SKETCHED BY   SHRYOCK.

THE FIRST PRESBYTERIAN CHURCH.

This church, Rev. W. F. V. Bartlett, pastor, is a new and handsome structure, with a tall and graceful spire, located on North Mill street. between Second and Church streets. The Presbyterians organized the first church established in Lexington, and 1884 is the centennial year of its existence. Colonel Robert Patterson, the founder of Lexington, was a member of this congregation, which first worshipped in a rude log cabin, on the southeastern corner of Walnut and Short, and he and other members frequently attended services with rifles in their hands, for the Christian pioneer of a hundred years ago had to literally "watch" (for Indians) as well as "pray." The earliest pastor of the church was the talented, but eccentric, Adam Rankin, who died while *en route* to the city of Jerusalem. Dr. James Blythe, a President of Transylvania University ; Rev. W. L. McCalla, Chaplain of the Navy of the Republic of Texas ; Rev. Nathan Hall, the powerful exhorter, and the able divine, Dr. R. J. Breckinridge, were pastors of this church.

THE SECOND PRESBYTERIAN CHURCH—Rev. George P. Wilson, pastor—is located on the east side of Market street, between Second and Church streets. It was for a time called "McChord Church," in honor of its firs pastor, the able, scholarly and eloquent James McChord, whose remains are interred beneath the pulpit. Dr. John C. Young, late President of Centre College, and Dr. Robert Davidson, author of the "History of the Presbyterian Church in Kentucky," were pastors of this church. The interior of the building is charming for its symmetry and elegance.

THE LEXINGTON LIBRARY.

Located on the corner of Market and Church Streets, is the oldest institution of its kind in the Western country, having been founded in 1795. It is more remarkable for the character than the number of the books it contains, abounding as it does in early and rare editions of works now scarcely attainable elsewhere for any consideration. Here the tourist can see the quaint old files of "The Kentucke Gazette," the first newspaper ever published in Kentucky. and the second one printed west of the Alleghany Mountains. It was established in Lexington by John Bradford in 1787 while this city was a frontier station, before Cincinnati was founded, and while this State was still a part of Virginia. Librarian, MISS CARRIE LEWINSKI.

WOOLEN MILLS.

Lexington presents an inviting field for the establishment of woollen mills, as she is the centre of a district which produces five or six million pounds of wool annually, and has but two factories, and they with limited capacity devoted entirely to the production of jeans, yarns and hosiery. Our grades of wool are principally quarter blood, medium, and Cotswold combings, with some fine Southdown, all of which, owing to the smoothness and culture of our lands and the large extent of clean blue-grass pasturage, is generally in superior condition. The shrinkage of our wool is much less than that of many other localities, and in the important item of price brings about the average of good Ohio wool. Men of enterprise, trained and experienced in this branch of industry, and with capital to back their skill, are badly needed here, and would be most cordially welcomed. Hundreds of looms should be in operation in Lexington turning out flannels, carpets, knit goods, blankets, satinets, cassimeres, and every variety of coatings and suitings.

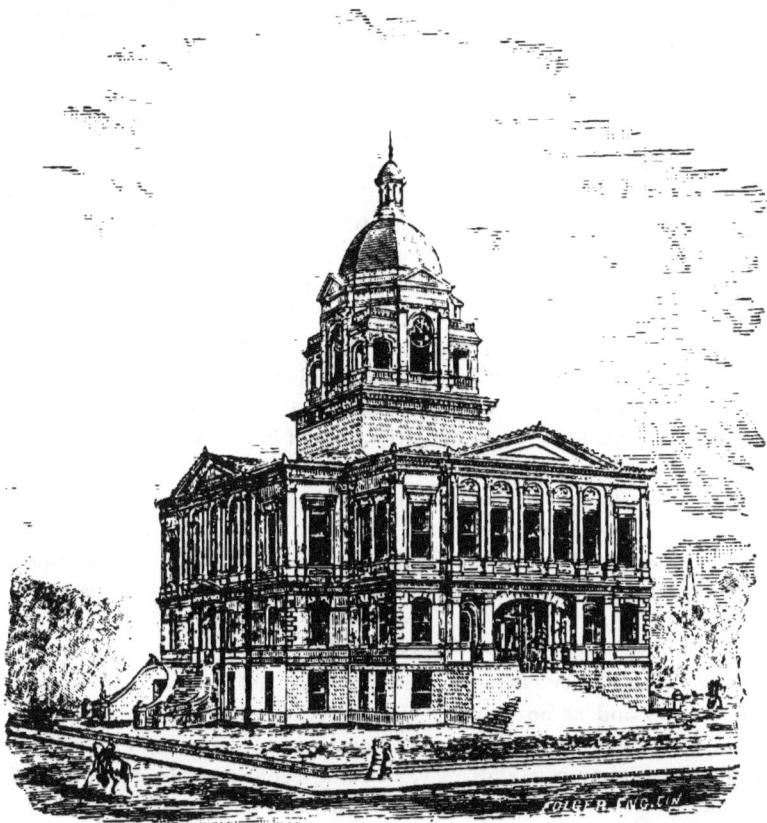

JOHNS,   PHOTO.

THE NEW COURT HOUSE.

[Its Memorable Site].

This handsome building is now in process of erection in the centre of
the public square, a spot that has been a Court House site for nearly a hundred years, and where many events of historic interest have occurred. In
the stone Court House erected here in 1788 those two great political leaders,
John Pope and Felix Grundy hotly discussed the merits of Federalism, and
from its steps in 1794 Gen. James Wilkinson, afterwards Commander in
Chief of the American Army, called for volunteers for Wayne's campaign
against the Indians. A quaint old edifice erected in 1806 preceded the one
now being built, and was rich in associations. In this house, in the summer

of 1807, took place the examining trial of the accomplished, but unfortunate, Blannerhassett, who had just been arrested in Lexington for complicity in the celebrated Burr conspiracy, and within its walls Clay and Barry, Wickliffe and Menifice, Tom, Marshall, Gen. Breckinridge, and a host of other distinguished orators made some of their most eloquent efforts. Amos Kendall, the right hand man of "Old Hickory," qualified as an attorney in this building. On its bench sat Judge Bledsoe, one of the most remarkable men of his day, and there, for the last time, pleaded the great lawyer, Joe Daviess, just before he fell so gallantly in the battle of Tippecanoe. Volunteers for the war of 1812 marched around it when they started for the bloody field of Raisin; "John Morgan's men" camped about it fifty years afterwards; its old bell rung a peal of triumph over the victory of Buena Vista, and often sounded the tocsin of alarm during the late terrible struggle between the States. The old house was once saved from destruction by fire by Confederate soldiers, when the city was held by General E. Kirby Smith. The new Court House fitly indicates the new era of progress upon which the old city has entered. The weather-beaten monument standing near the Court House was erected nearly half a century ago to a distinguished citizen of Lexington and Democratic leader, William T. Barry, who was successively United States Senator, Postmaster General, and Minister to Spain.

LEXINGTON'S PROGRESS.

At no time in fifty years has this city increased so rapidly in population as at present, and at no equal period have there been so many buildings erected. The demand for business houses and residences is large and unabating, the mechanics are all busy, a strong feeling in favor of the establishment and fostering of manufactories exists, new and substantial enterprises have been successfully inaugurated, and the once sleepy city is waking up and rapidly imbibing the spirit and push of a three-year old Western town.

RESIDENCES AND MERCHANDISE.

There are two features of Lexington that continually attract the attention of strangers—one is the size and elegance of the private residences and the tasteful profusion of flowers and shrubbery about them, and the other is the superior quality of the goods on sale in the stores. There is probably no place of its size in this country whose trade requires a finer line of merchandise than Lexington. An immense amount of the most elegant and expensive kinds of dry goods, furniture, carpets, jewelry, pianos, clothing, table ware &c, is disposed of annually. Both features named indicate the culture and the wealth of the community.

THE BIRTHPLACE OF WESTERN MASONRY.

The Masonic Hall, on the corner of Short and Walnut streets, is an object of interest to strangers of the "mystic tie" from the fact that it occupies the spot upon which was established the first lodge of Freemasons organized in the now mighty empire of the West. This lodge, originally called "No. 25," but afterward named "No. 1," was chartered by the Grand Lodge of Virginia on the 17th of November, 1788, while Lexington was only a little frontier post of the Old Diminion and Cincinnati nothing but a howling wil-

derness. Its original charter, yellow with age, is still to be seen in this city- Colonel Joe Daviess, one of the ablest lawyers of his time, and the prose. cutor of Aaron Burr, was a member of this lodge, and was the Grand Master of Kentucky when he fell in the battle of Tippecanoe, November 7th, 1811, and an imposing funeral ceremonial was performed in his honor by the Grand Lodge at its meeting in Lexington the following summer. The present hall was used as a military hospital during the late war between the States. (See list of Masonic lodges).

RUSSELL'S CAVE,

Situated about six miles north of Lexington, on the Russell road, is an object of worthy of attention, as is also the region about it. In this picturesque locality the tourist can not only observe the singular spectacle of a cave from which issues a subterranean stream of sufficient volume to turn a mill, but he can inspect the remains of a circular fort attributed to the Mound Builders, the mysterious race which preceded the Indians ages ago in the unknown past of America.

ELMENDORF STUD FARM.

[*Late "Preakness" Stud.*]

This well-known farm, the property of Mr. D. Swigert, is situated on the waters of North Elkhorn, six miles from Lexington on the Maysville pike, and comprises 544 acres in grass. Its fine barns, paddocks and lots give accommodations to a stud of eighty-five thoroughbred mares and four thoroughbred stallions, including Prince Charlie, the famous English race-horse just bought and imported, and the winner of twenty-five races; Virgil, sire of Hindoo, one of the best racers America has ever known; Imp. Glenelg, sire of the noted mare, Ferida, and Lever, the sire of Mahlstick, Apollo, &c. There are more Lexington and Australian mares in this stud than in any other establishment in the world. This stud breeds and sells annually by auction all produce as yearlings. At the last sale forty-four thoroughbred yearlings realized $47,930. At the next annual sale, which occurs in May, 1884, forty-seven yearlings will be sold to the highest bidder and Elmendorf will be the point of attraction for buyers from many parts of the country. Mr. Swigert's post-office is Muir, Fayette Co., Ky.

NEWSPAPER OFFICES.

Press (Daily and Weekly), by H. T. Duncan, Cheapside.

Transcript (Daily and Weekly), by D. E. Caldwell, corner Upper and Church.

Evening News (Daily and Weekly), by T. A. Flannelly, in Odd Fellows' Temple, East Main street.

Kentucky Advertiser (Daily and Weekly), by I. C. Montfort, East Main, nearly opposite Phœnix Hotel.

Kentucky Gazette (Semi-Weekly and Weekly), by H. H. Gratz, Cheapside.

Live Stock Record (Weekly), bv B. G. Bruce. Jordan's Row.

Observer (Sunday), by J. O. Hodges, Jr., Main, between Upper and Limestone.

Apostolic Times (Religious Weekly), by B. H. Cozine, Market, between Short and Church.

Hamilton College Monthly, college building, Broadway.

Kentucky Republican (Weekly), by H. Scroggins (colored), East Vine.

MULLEN.   PHOTO.

SCOTT'S BLOCK.

(Site of the first capitol of Kentucky).

Stands on the east side of Main street, between Mill and Broadway, and occupies the site of a two-story log house of the regular old pioneer type, in
which, on the fourth of June, 1792, commenced the first session of the Kentucky Legislature and the organization of the State Government. On the
sixth of June both houses assembled in the Senate chamber of the State
House, and at twelve o'clock Governor Shelby entered and delivered his mes-
sage in person, preceded and followed by courtly courtesies, which were in
striking contrast with the simple surroundings of the backwoods settlement.
The next year the State Capitol was removed to Frankfort, much to the in-
dignation of Lexington, which was then the most important town on the
frontier.   It is confidently expected by many that the central location of Lexington, her extensive railroad communications, fine hotel facilities, and other
important advantages, will cause her to become again the capital of the State.

A CHANCE FOR MECHANICS.

Competent and reliable mechanics are offered many and strong induce-ments to settle in Lexington. The city is growing rapidly, having progressed more in the past two years than in any previous ten in half a century. There is plenty of work to do and wages are good. Here industrious work-men are not compelled to crowd their families into the teeming upper stories of health-destroying hives with neither privacy nor domestic liberty, to con-sort with disease and vice in a stifling atmosphere of foul courts and narrow streets. The miserable eastern tenement-house system is practically un-known and unnecessary. Here, where there is plenty of room for all, the mechanic can have his family in a one story cottage, with yard and reasonable conveniences, at as cheap a rate, everything considered, as the rent asked for the inferior tenement homes abounding in crowded cities. Building lots in the suburbs can be bought cheap, and building lumber can be obtained at nearly half the price asked in eastern markets. Good coal is low priced here the whole year round ; the necessaries of life are abundant and sell at reasonable rates; the city schools which are finely conducted offer all their advantages free of charge; benevolent orders are numerous and in good condition; the mild climate admits of open air labor throughout the year; the healthfulness of the city is one of its special characteristics; churches and Sunday-schools abound, and a cordial invitation to come and settle among us is extended to all worthy and thrifty mechanics, no matter what their nationality, religious creed, or political opinions.

———

SUBURBAN ATTRACTIONS.

No stranger can do justice to Lexington and vicinity without inspecting her suburban attractions. These are quickly reached by superb turnpikes which extend from the Blue Grass Capitol in every direction, affording the visitor exhilarating drives past noted old places, and woodlands and blue grass pastures; by farms famous for their yields of corn, and wheat, and hemp, and tobacco, and through scenes of pastoral beauty and fertility that would lend a grace even to the noted landscapes of Old England. Stables, and paddocks, and training tracks, and flocks, and herds, meet the eye on every hand, reminding the tourist that he is in the midst of a region, which, for stock raising, is unsurpassed upon the face of the earth—a superiority derived from the limestone formation underlying the soil, which is at once the greatest gift, and the most striking peculiarity of the blue grass country.

ASHLAND,

The home of Henry Clay, and one of our national shrines, is on the Richmond road, just beyond the city limits. With it the tourist is never disappointed, for not only are its natural charms equal to its historic associations, but the general appearance of the old homestead is substantially the same as during the lifetime of "the Great Commoner." The locust avenue, the favorite walk of Mr. Clay ; the catalpas which he planted, and which bowed over him when he was borne to his last resting place; the dairy used by

Mrs. Clay for half a century; the old negro cabins, and the pigeon houses are still as they were when the great orator swayed multitudes with his wonderful eloquence. The beautiful woodwork of the family residence was made from the ash trees which grew upon the farm and gave the place its very appropriate name. Mr. Clay once said of his Blue Grass home, "I occupy as good a farm as Moses would have found had he reached the Promised Land, and Ashland has been acquired not by hereditary descent, but by my own labor." Here the afterwards distinguished Amos Kendall started in life as the tutor of the children of the eminent statesman, who had himself been at one time only "the mill-boy of the slashes." Here were entertained with simple, but abundant, hospitality, Daniel Webster, the Earl of Derby, General Bertrand, Harriet Martineau, Van Buren, and a host of others equally noted. Here, in the summer of 1847, the worn and disappointed leader was baptized according to the forms of the Episcopal Church, and here, on the 10th of July, 1852, amid the sables of woe, the tolling of bells, the sad booming of minute guns, and surrounded by a vast concourse of sorrowing friends, his weary body rested for the last time before it was entombed. During the late war a part of Ashland was the scene of one of John Morgan's sudden dashes, in which he surprised and captured a Federal command. In 1866 the place was sold to Kentucky University, which recently disposed of it to Maj. H. C. McDowell, whose wife is a granddaughter of Mr. Clay. The farm of John M. Clay, Esq., the only surviving child of "Harry of the West," adjoins Ashland, of which it was a part in his father's lifetime.

A LOCATION FOR TOBACCO FACTORIES.

It would be hard to exaggerate the claims of Lexington as a place for the location of tobacco factories. In the first place, she is in the very heart of the greatest tobacco growing State in the Union. In 1880, out of a total of 473,107,573 lbs. of tobacco, Kentucky produced 171,121,134 lbs., and the plant is being so extensively cultivated around this city that the averages for 1883 will be at least double that of any preceding year, giving the Blue Grass Region the largest yield per acre of any part of the United States, and showing that it is destined to be the leading tobacco district of the world. The White Burley, which is so successfully and profitably raised here, is especially adapted to plug and cutting manufacture, and thus strongly commends itself to enterprising men with an eye to business. The prospects of a future market are flattering. The crop of the whole country for this year being 18,000 hhds. less than crops of the three years preceding, the crude tobacco will be valuable next season, and the scarcity of goods will increase the profits of the manufacturing interests There is no obstacle of any kind whatever to the successful establishment and profitable conduct of tobacco factories at this place, for we have the crude material, water, cheap fuel, cheap labor, and all the railroad facilities necessary for transportation, and they would be welcomed, as affording opportunities for the employment of unoccupied boys, whose time could thus be made valuable, as hand labor s the thing most needed in such factories. A little energy on the part of capitalists would make Lexington celebrated for her chewing and smoking tobacco, and give employment to several thousand men and boys.

IOHNS. PHOTO.

THE FIRST BAPTIST CHURCH.

This commodious edifice is located on Short street, west of Spring It occupies a memorable spot, for it stands in the midst of the first burying ground of the early settlers of Lexington, where rest the ashes of pioneers slain by the Indians when this city was a mere stockade in the savage wilderness. There was an infant congregation of Baptists in Lexington as early as 1786, and it enjoyed the ministrations of the noted Elder Lewis Craig, who was imprisoned in Virginia for preaching contrary to law, and who, in 1783, organized a Baptist Church at South Elkhorn, near this city, which was the first worshipping assembly of any kind established in Kentucky.

THE UPPER STREET BAPTIST CHURCH—REV. J. J. Taylor, Pastor— Stands on the corner of Upper and Church streets. This tasteful building was dedicated in 1877.

FIRST BAPTIST (colored), Rev. S. P. Young, Pastor, corner Dewees and Short streets.

EVERGREEN BAPTIST (colored), Rev. John Morgan, Pastor, Market street, between Seventh and corporation line.

INDEPENDENT BAPTIST (colored), Rev. Evans, Pastor, corner Main and Merino.

PLEASANT GREEN BAPTIST (colored), Rev. Morris Bell, Pastor, corner Maxwell and Lower.

ENGINE HOUSE BAPTIST, (colored), Rev. James Parrish, Pastor, Limestone, between High and Water.

THE COLORED PEOPLE AND NEGRO JAILS.

The negroes of Lexington, light hearted, careless and numerous, and with their peculiar characteristics of speech and manner, are always a novelty to strangers unused to the race. Such visitors could not witness a much more striking sight than a parade by a colored secret society of this city but if he would more closely observe these remarkable people he should attend services in one of their handsome churches (see lists elsewhere), and visit their crowded schools and unique settlements. The colored agricultural association here is a success and a credit to the race. In ante-bellum days there were several negro trading establishments in Lexington which were provided with jails and auction rooms where slaves were kept for sale and hire. Three of these houses were in the neighborhood of the present Post-Office. One was on the site of Lell's Hall, and was used during the war as a Federal Provost Marshall's office, and another on Broadway, now occupied by physicians, became a Confederate hospital.

HIGH BRIDGE.

A ride of thirty minutes over the Cincinnati Southern Railway brings the traveler to the Kentucky River, and to the highest pier bridge in the world, the rails being two hundred and seventy-six feet above the bed of the stream. This marvel of engineering skill is well placed, for it stands in the midst of some of the grandest and most picturesque scenery on this continent. The towering cliffs, the battlemented crags, the hoary rocks, and splendid foliage, and the awful canon, through which deep down the beautiful river runs, make up a scene so full of natural charms as to require no artificial attractions, such as embellish the Hudson, to excite the unbounded admiration of the beholder.

MULLEN

THE GRAND STAND LEXINGTON FAIR GROUNDS.

PHOTO.

THE FAIR GROUNDS.

The splendid grounds of the Kentucky Agricultural and Mechanical Association, with their noble forest trees, picturesque buildings and fine drives and views, are just within the suburban limits of South Broadway, and are readily reached by the street cars. The spacious "Crescent," or Grand Stand, will hold ten thousand people, the trotting track is not surpassed by any on this continent, and the floral hall, reception rooms, and stabling facilities are first-class. The Fair always commences about the last of August and is one of the most important and successful in this country. Its immense crowds, magnificent live stock, and superb aggregation of all the important products and attractions of the Blue Grass Region afford the tourist his best chance to not only see for himself whether the much-vaunted resources of this fertile district are overestimated, but to observe old Kentucky life and manners in one of its most charming and animated phases. The Fair is located in the center of the finest stock-raising region on the globe, and it is no idle boast to say that its displays of thoroughbred race horses, fast trotters, pure-bred Short-horn and Alderney cattle, Southdown and Cotswold sheep, superior hogs and other live stock, are the grandest to be seen in this country. The first importation of improved stock to this region was made as early as 1785, and horse and cattle shows were held at Lexington before the commencement of the present century. The President of the Association is W. H. Gentry ; Secretary, H. P. Kinkead.

RAILROAD DEPOTS.

Big Sandy (Chesapeake and Ohio), rear of Phœnix Hotel

Kentucky Central, rear of Phœnix Hotel.

Louisville, Cincinnati and Lexington (Louisville and Nashville), corner Mill and Water streets.

Cincinnati Southern (C., N. O. and T P.), South Broadway.

The road now known as the "Louisville, Cincinnati and Lexington" was chartered as the "Lexington and Ohio," and enjoys the distinction of being the first railroad built in the West, and one of the first built in America. It was incorporated January 27th, 1830. The strap iron rails were soldered to stone sills, which were laid lengthwise. It is believed that the first locomotive made in the United States ran over this road. It was invented by Thomas Barlow, of Lexington, as early as 1827, and was also built in Lexington.

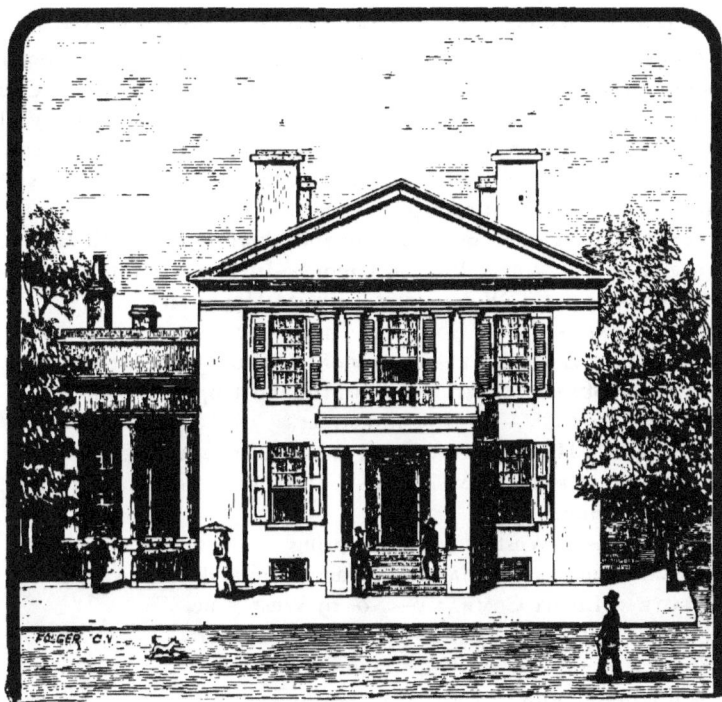

THE NORTHERN BANK OF KENTUCKY.

This venerable and solid-looking building, with a capital of $1,813,900, is located on the corner of Short and Market, fronting Cheapside. It was erected and first occupied by the Lexington branch of the United States Bank, and was just completed, in 1832, when President Jackson visited the city. Tradition says that the irreverant old hero caught a glimpse of the building as he was on his way to church the Sunday after his arrival, and muttering "By the Eternal!" brought his cane down upon the pavement with a thundering rap. Shortly after this the institution, so emphatically doomed, ceased to exist, and the Northern Bank, established in 1835, wound up the concern. The "old Northern," which has for so many years been noted throughout the Union for its able management, prosperity and high character, has been for a quarter of a century under the presidency of the distinguished Madison C. Johnson, and for nearly half a century has profited by his sagacity as director. The name of this profound jurist and financier is inseparably connected with the Northern Bank. It is his monument.

PUBLIC BUILDINGS AND PROMINENT PLACES.

COUNTY OFFICES.—A new Court House being in process of erection, the county offices are temporarily stationed as follows, viz : Office of County Judge over Second National Bank, cor. Short and Cheapside; County Clerk, on Short street, between Cheapside and Upper ; Circuit Court room and Circuit Clerk, in Masonic Hall, corner of Walnut and Short; Sheriff's office, in Court House yard, fronting Upper street.

POSTOFFICE.—Corner of Broadway and Short.—H. K. Milward, P. M.

TELEGRAPH OFFICE (Western Union)—In Phœnix Hotel.

MARKET HOUSE.—Water street, between Upper and Vine.

COUNTY JAIL—Corner Short and Limestone.

TELEPHONE EXCHANGE.—Corner of Main and Cheapside.

WATCH HOUSE.—Water, between Mill and Upper.

ORPHAN ASYLUM.—West Third street.

ST. JOSEPH'S HOSPITAL.—Second street, near Jefferson.

ARMORY OF LEXINGTON GUARDS.—In Jackson Hall, corner Limestone and Water.

GAS WORKS.—West Main, near Spring

ADAMS EXPRESS COMPANY—Corner Main and Broadway.

ELECTRIC LIGHT COMPANY—No. 19 West Vine.

HOME OF THE FRIENDLESS—No. 80 West Short.

WORK HOUSE—Corner Upper and Bolivar.

FIRE DEPARTMENT—East Short street.

CITY DISPENSARY—Water street, between Mill and Upper.

ST. CATHERINE'S ACADEMY—North Limestone.

CHRIST CHURCH SEMINARY—Maxwell, near Limestone.

INDUSTRIAL SCHOOL—In No. 3 City School Building, corner Mill and Maxwell.

CHURCH HOME. EPISCOPAL—Corner Walnut and Winchester.

CATHOLIC CEMETERY—South side of West Main, at Corporation line.

PRESBYTERIAN CEMETERY—Sixth, between Limestone and Upper.

EPISCOPAL CEMETERY—North side of Third Street, West of Dewees.

HOTELS.

PHŒNIX—Corner Main and Limestone.

ASHLAND HOUSE—Short, between Mill and Broadway.

ST. NICHOLAS—East Main, near Limestone.

FLORENTINE—East Main, near Limestone.

ALEXANDER HOUSE—East Short, near Limestone.

FAYETTE HOUSE—East Short, near Limestone.

THE CLAY MONUMENT.

The most prominent object in the Lexington Cemetery is the monument erected in honor of Henry Clay. It is one hundred and twenty feet in height; is built of the beautiful limestone of this State, popularly known as "Kentucky marble," and consists of an elegant Corinthian column rising from a massive sub-base of the Egyptian style, and surmounted by a statue of the great orator. A marble sarcophagus in the vaulted chamber of the

monument contains the last mortal remains of "Harry of the West," and is plainly visible through the fretted door. Upon the side of the coffin is chiseled the solemn and memorable declaration of Mr. Clay made in his address on retiring from the United States Senate in 1842: "I can with unshaken confidence appeal to the Divine Arbiter for the truth of the declaration that I have been influenced by no impure purpose, no personal motive, have sought no personal aggrandizement; but in all my public acts I have had a sole and single eye, and a warm, devoted heart, directed and dedicated to what in my best judgment I believed to be the true interests of my country." Another marble sarcophagus rests near that of the departed statesman and contains the remains of his wife, Mrs. Lucretia Clay, who survived her husband twelve years, dying in 1864, aged eighty-three. Mr. Clay's mother and other members of his family are buried in another part of the cemetery. The corner stone of this monument was laid with imposing ceremonies on the 4th of July, 1857. Mr. Clay died on the 29th day of June, 1852, in the seventy-sixth year of his age.

SKILLED LABOR.

The thinking people of Lexington are warmly disposed in favor of skilled labor, and are inclined to welcome with especial pleasure the establishment of any and all manufactories employing such labor. They realize the fact that a large accession of skilled workmen would be one of the greatest blessing that could befall this city, not simply because they are necessary to the full development of our manufacturing interests, but because they make intelligent, law abiding, valuable citizens, and are capable of instructing our boys and girls in the manifold branches of the most important mechanic arts. Such manufacturies would not only "pay" in a pecuniary sense, but they would "pay" most abundantly as training schools for the idle and unemployed who would thus be made useful and productive members of the community. These are the only educational establishments that Lexington lacks; the kind she needs most of all ; the kind that self-preservation demands she must have, and the ones that the thoughtful and intelligent are most disposed to foster and encourage. The best people of this city would gladly welcome an inpouring of skilled workmen regardless of their politics or nativity. The old, silly and senseless prejudice against mechanical pursuits is exploded, and lingers only in the shallow pates of effeminate "dudes" and witless fops, ten thousand of whom, in the estimation of sensible people, are not worth one competent and thrifty workman. We need establishments where the children of the city, male and female, may learn to be self-supporting by being trained to occupations which develop skill, taste and talent, such as the manufacture of the various parts of watches, of optical, dental and surgical instruments, hardware, silverware, fine machinery, artistic pottery, fire-arms, jewelry, artificial flowers, gold leaf and dental foil, chemicals, paints, musical instruments, perfumery, stationery, brushes, fancy goods, decorative work on glass, pottery, and textile fabrics, and in the prosecution of such pursuits as silver-plating, wood carving, bronze work, engraving, lithographing, &c. The rapidly developing South wants all these things, and Lexington, right at her portals, is the very place for their manufacture, and the point from which they could the most easily be distributed.

STABLE AT FAIRLAWN.

FAIRLAWN.—One of the most noted and extensive establishments in this country devoted to the rearing of high-bred trotting stock is Fairlawn, the property of Gen. W. T. Withers, at the extremity of North Broadway, and as such is constantly sought out by the multitude of horsemen and buyers of fine stock who visit Lexington. The house, with its Southern air and amplitude, the picturesque lawn, and the undulating pastures and blue grass paddocks teeming with trotters, make up a sight that charms the stranger's eye. The principal stable, with its stained glass windows, lofty tower and complete arrangements, is one of the largest and handsomest of its kind in existence, and is alone worth a visit to see. But the pre-eminent feature of Fairlawn is its splendid stud, at the head of which stands the peerless "Almont 33," by Alexander's Abdallah 15; dam Sallie Anderson, by Mambrino Chief 11; grandam Kate, by Pilot, Jr., 12. Twenty-one of the sons and daughters of Almont now have records of 2:30 or better, and four of them have records below 2:20.   In 1883 Mr. W. H. Vanderbilt's team of Aldine (by Almont) and Maud S.. driven in wagon by Mr. V. himself, trotted in public in 2:15¼, the fastest double team to date.   Besides Almont there can be seen at Fairlawn the celebrated trotting stallions Happy Medium 400, by Rysdyk's Hambletonian; dam the noted trotting mare Princess, with seventeen of his produce with records below 2:30 ; Aberdeen. 27, also by Rysdyk's Hambletonian ; dam the great trotting mare Widow Machree, by Seeley's American Star, with nine of his sons and daughters with records below 2:28½, two being below 2:20 ; and Ethan Allen 473, with six of his produce with records below 2:30.   These great stallions, and the one hundred and twenty head of brood-mares owned at Fairlawn, with their numerous produce, should be seen by all visitors to the Blue Grass capital.   It is hardly necessary to add that Fairlawn trotters are sold and shipped to all parts of the world.

THE KENTUCKY UNION RAILWAY

Has its headquarters on Cheapside, corner of Main street; T. J. Megibben President and A. G. P. Dodge Vice President.   This road, which is now in process of construction, is destined to exert a powerful influence for good upon the future growth and prosperity of Lexington, will be her shortest route to the unsurpassed coal, iron and timber resources of our neighboring district of Eastern Kentucky, and will form a new trunk line to the Atlantic seaboard.   It will bring to Lexington the natural treasures that lie almost at her threshold from a region called by Professor Shaler, of Harvard University, "the richest field of mineral wealth known in any country."   He says further : "The eastern coal field of Kentucky contains 844 square miles of coal area more than Great Britain, nearly double that of Spain, and more than three times greater than that of France.   Many of the coals are equal to, or superior to, the best Pittsburg, and the best of these contain several per cent. less ashes and more fixed carbon than the Youghiogheny coal. The cannel coal field of Eastern Kentucky probably covers an area of over three thousand square miles, and is much the largest known to me."   Prof. Proctor, State Geologist, says : "In no region of the United States can iron be produced cheaper."   Engineer W. A. Gunn, referring to the iron ores on this line, says : "They are considered fully equal to Lake Superior and Iron Mountain ores, so largely used in the North," and Engineer William McCloy declares, "I have never seen a region where facilities for easy and cheap mining so greatly abound."   The entire mountains on either side of Red River are filled with iron of the most superior quality, from which is made the celebrated "Red River Car Wheel Iron."   There is no large mine in the United States equal to it. Prof. Shaler says : "The timber in the belt of country to be traversed by this line constitutes the finest forest of virgin hard wood known to me in this country," a declaration affirmed by Mr. Gunn, who declares that "besides the Red River supply of timber the Kentucky River region is over four times as large, and here are the finest walnut, poplar, oak, hickory, maple, ash, cherry, locust, chestnut, oak, etc., to be found in any country." Fine building stone, valuable lithographic stone, tile clays and fire clays also abound along the line of this road. The Union Railway company owns about 500,000 acres of land in the rich sections above described, and Messrs. J. M. Thomas and Benjamin Crawford are in charge o the Lands Department.

SKETCHED BY   LUNDIN.

CENTENARY METHODIST EPISCOPAL CHURCH.

This church, Rev. Wm. McAfee, Pastor, stands on the corner of Broadway and Church Streets. The church was organized in the centennial year of Methodism in this country, and was named in memory of that interesting event. The building is an ornament to the city, and though only dedicated in 1870 shelters one of our most prosperous and active congregations.

THE HILL STREET METHODIST CHURCH (South)—Rev. W. S. Noland, Pastor—is on High Street, near Upper, and has just been handsomely improved. This is a memorable region to Methodists, for the first church built in Kentucky (1787) was erected at Masterson's Station (Dr. Spurr's), about five miles northwest of this city, and there also in 1790 the first annual State Conference was held with the noted Bishop Asbury as presiding officer. The Lexington Church was estsblished in 1789 by the impassioned and self-sacrificing Francis Poythress. The Hill Street Church was dedicated in 1842 by the then President of Transylvania University, the eloquent Bishop Bascom, of whom Henry Clay said: "He is the greatest natural orator I ever heard." In the rear of the building is the legendary graveyard of the German Lutheran Church, long since extinct, which occupied the spot nearly a hundred years ago.

THE ASBURY METHODIST CHURCH (Colored)——Rev. W. H. Evans, Pastor—Water Street, west of Limestone.

ST. PAUL'S (Colored)—Rev. R. Whitman, Pastor—Upper Street, between Third and Mechanic.

GUNN'S CHAPEL (Colored)—Rev. J. W. Thomas, Pastor—North end of Dewees Street.

DICTATOR.

One of the attractions of Lexington, to lovers of the horse, is the superb trotting sire, Dictator, the head of Maj McDowell's stud, at "Ashland," the home of Henry Clay. Dictator is the full brother of Dexter. He is the sire of Jay-Eye-See, with a five-year old record of 2:14; of Phallas, with a six-year old stallion record of 2:15½, and of Director, with a six-year old stallion record of 2:17. No other sire has yet produced three horses with records as good as 2:17; nor produced two with records below 2:16. These and others of his get have shown not only wonderful speed, but more wonderful endurance. Although Dictator is in his twenty-first year, the price paid for him was $25,000, and the opinion is that he was fully worth it. Kentucky could not afford to let such a horse be taken from the State.

JOHNS,   PHOTO.

THE CITY HALL.

This new and extensive building occupies an entire block, between Upper and Limestone, and includes the office of the Mayor, the City Council
Chamber, Recorder's Court Room, and quarters of various city officers. The
ground floor is used for the market. The principal officers of the City Government are

MAYOR—C. M. JOHNSON.

COUNCIL.

First Ward.	Third Ward.
JAMES McCORMICK.	J. R. GRAVES.
W. H. MAY.	B. J. TREACY.
MOSES KAUFMAN.	F. WATERS.
Second Ward.	Fourth Ward.
J. M. GRAVES.	JOHN BOYD.
W. S. McCHESNEY.	JOHN W. BERKLEY.
RICHARD GARLAND.	TEDDY MEHAN.

Treasurer—J. M. TANNER.
Collector—D. D. LAUDEMAN.
Assessor—M. C. FOUSHEE.

WAR POINTS.

Though Lexington was occupied by the Federal forces during most of the late war, it was repeatedly threatened by the Confederates, and fell into their hands no less than three times. The city, therefore, is full of associations of the exciting days when it was "under two flags," and there are but few places in it that are not connected in some way with memorable events and stirring deeds. Morrison College and the Masonic Hall sheltered hundreds of sick and wounded and dying soldiers. The trotting track was the scene of several awful military executions. It was in front of the Phœnix Hotel that General Nelson mounted when he dashed out on his terrific ride to assume command at the disastrous battle of Richmond, and the same hotel was afterwards the headquarters of the Confederate Generals Bragg and Kirby Smith. Blood was shed at Ashland, where a body of Federals were surprised and captured by John Morgan, whose headquarters during the Confederate occupation were in the building on Upper street in, which the office of the Live Stock Record is located. The site of the State College was a favorite camping ground of both armies. Fort Clay, erected by Gen. Q. A. Gilmore, was on the Versailles turnpike, overlooking the Southern Railroad. Gen. Burbridge used as his headquarters the residence on the corner of Second and Upper, now occupied by Mrs. Dudley. Of the several Federal military prisons, two are conspicuous for their tragic associations. One is the building on Water street, nearly opposite the Watch House, and partially cased with iron, and the other is the present jail, on the corner of Short and Limestone. From both condemned Confederate soldiers went forth to execution.

CHEESE FACTORIES WANTED.

If there is a spot on the face of the earth where factories for the making cheese and also condensed milk ought to succeed it is at Lexington. We have the finest of cows in countless numbers, the best grass in the world, and green the whole year round, and for cooling purposes have cold spring water in unusual abundance, and an inexhaustable ice supply. Milk can be had here cheaper than in the famous cheese district of New York, and of a quality to produce the best cheese that can be made. With sufficient capital an experienced management and hands trained to the work, success is assured. The same may be said of condensed milk, and as the principal market for that article is the South, the advantages of Lexington as a distributing point will be at once preceived.

ALMONT (HEAD OF THE FAIRLAWN STUD).

DISTANCES

FROM LEXINGTON TO NEIGHBORING TOWNS.

Lexington, being the central city and metropolis of the Blue Grass Region, is surrounded by flourishing towns and interesting places, with all of which she is in direct and easy communication, either by her railroads or numerous and splendid turnpikes. The following is a list of the principal places near the city, and their distances from it, viz:

Georgetown	on Cincinnati Southern Railway	12	Miles.
Nicholasville	" " " " " "	12	"
Camp Nelson	" " " " " "	18	"
High Bridge	" " " " " "	20	"
Shakertown	" " " " " "	22	"
Harrodsburg	" " " " " "	34	"
Danville	" " " " " "	35	"
Spring Station	Louisville & Nashville "	20	"
Midway	" " " " " " "	14	"
Frankfort	" " " " " " "	28	"
Winchester	Chesapeake & Ohio "	18	"
Mt. Sterling	" " " " " "	34	"
Paris	Kentucky Central "	19	"
Cynthiana	" " " " " "	34	"
Carlisle	" " " " " "	36	"
Richmond	" " " " " "	40	"
" "	by turnpike	26	"
Versailles	" "	12	"
Harrodsburg	" "	35	"

No drives leading out from Lexington afford the tourist finer views of grand and picturesque scenery than the macadamized roads to Harrodsburg and Richmond. The site of Boonesboro, the famous fort established by Daniel Boone, in 1775, and which was attacked three times by the Indians, and whose thrilling and romantic experiences have been so often celebrated in story and in song, is on the Kentucky river, in Madison county, and is most conveniently reached by way of Winchester, from which it is only nine miles distant by turnpike.

IRON ORE AND CHEAP COAL.

Thousands of car loads of iron ore of the best quality annually pass through Lexington for distant points. Every pound of it ought to stop right here and be manufactured into locomotives, car wheels, boilers, store fronts,

hollow ware, castings and everything that is made of iron.   We can furnish
manufacturers with good lump coal, delivered at 8½ cents per bushel, No.
2 nut at 8 cents, and slack at 3 cents, which is as cheap as it can be had at
Louisville or Cincinnati, and our nearness to the mines cuts off a big item in
the shape of freight charges and transportation.   We need works and shops
for the manufacture of iron into a hundred shapes, and Lexington offers one
of the best fields in the West or South for their location.

JOHNS,   PHOTO.

THE CONFEDERATE MONUMENT

Is an object of interest to strangers.   It stands in the Lexington Cemetery,
and was erected by the Southern ladies of this city to the memory of the
Confederate soldiers whose graves surround it.   Frank Leslie's Illustrated
Newspaper said of it: "This monument. though excelled by others in size,
is probably the most perfect thing of its kind in the South, and viewed under
the influence of its surroundings and associations, presents a picture which
challenges criticism.   In the midst of several concentric circles of soldiers'

graves rises a rocky mound, upon which, represented in pure Carrara marble, stands the solitary trunk of a blasted tree, which, with its two naked arms, looms boldly up against a background of green elms and pines in the form of a natural cross. Resting against the rugged base is a nameless scroll and a broken sword, and clustered about them are luxuriant Southern foliage and vines. Planted at the foot of the cross is the shivered staff, which once upheld the Conquered Banner; but the flag has fallen to rise no more, and its stricken folds, caught by the arms of the cross, but with the stars and bars still showing, droop as lifeless as the martial forms which are moldering around. This monument exhibits in its design one of the highest qualities of true art, for it tells its own story—the tragic story of the Lost Cause—without the use of a single word upon its front. It is a poem in stone."

BANKS.

Not the least of the inducements offered by Lexington, to responsible parties, to locate in the city, are the abundant facilities its banks give for the transaction of business. There are eight prosperous banks in Lexington, representing a capital and surplus of between three and four millions of dollars. They are located as follows, viz:

DAVID A. SAYRE & CO., (private,) E. D. Sayre, Sr., and J. W. Sayre; N. E. corner Mill and Short. This is the oldest banking establishment in the city, having been founded in 1823, by the late David A. Sayre. The house was built by U. S. Senator John Pope, the distinguished one.armed competitor of Mr. Clay.

NORTHERN BANK OF KENTUCKY, (State), M. C. Johnson, president; W. D. Boswell, cashier; corner Market and Short. Capital $1,813,900,

FIRST NATIONAL BANK, A. S Winston, president; Thos. Mitchell, cashier: Short, between Market and Upper. Capital $400,000.

SECOND NATIONAL BANK, D. H. James, President; W. D. Nicholas, cashier; corner Cheapside and Short. Capital $100,000.

THIRD NATIONAL BANK, J. W. Berkley, president; O. Lee Bradley, cashier; corner Short and Upper, (late Grinstead & Bradley's Bank). Capital $100,000.

LEXINGTON CITY NATIONAL BANK, R. P. Stoll, president; James M. Graves, cashier; corner Main and Cheapside. Capital $200,000.

FAYETTE NATIONAL BANK, Squire Bassett, president; R. S. Bullock, cashier; corner Main and Upper. Capital $300,000.

NATIONAL EXCHANGE BANK, J. B. Wilgus, president; W. Bright, cashier; Main near Mill. Capital $100,000.

HAMILTON FEMALE COLLEGE.

HAMILTON FEMALE COLLEGE.

This institution occupies an elevated site on North Broadway, near Fourth, and is noticeable, not only from the fact that it is one of the most flourishing female schools in the Mississippi Valley, but for the character of its general equipment. The large four-story building, which contains over a hundred apartments, is provided with music halls, a chapel, gymnasium, laboratory, &c.; is warmed by steam, lighted with gas, and is supplied with hot and cold water, bathing facilities, and other comforts and conveniences. The faculty which is very full and able, is composed of fifteen members, with the experienced and efficient Prof. J. T. Patterson as President, and the institution is under the control and patronage of the Christian Church. It is a home as well as a first-class school. The College was named in honor of Mr. William Hamilton, of Woodford County, Ky., who donated $10,000 to it; and thus entered the list of Lexington's public benefactors, who, like Morrison, have helped to make this city one of the greatest educational points in this country.

A HINT TO MANUFACTURERS.

The attention of parties seeking a location for manufacturing enterprises is called to the important fact that Lexington is a railroad centre; that sixty or seventy passenger and freight trains arrive and depart here daily, and that quick and easy communication is had with all parts of the country. Especial stress is laid upon the fact that we have three competing lines to the South, which is so rapidly advancing in population, wealth and enterprise, and is already one of the finest markets for manufactured articles in the world. Enormous resources of raw material for manufacturing are right at Lexington's door; we have inexhaustable supplies of the cheapest and best coal on the market, and our facilities for distributing manufactured goods at low rates through a vast Southern territory are unsurpassed. These are not mere sounding assertions, but facts that will bear investigation. The distinguished Prof. Shaler, of Harvard University, says on this point:

"There are few agricultural regions of this country where so large a proportions of the products are calculated to furnish eastward freights. This region is naturally well fitted to become the seat of those extensive industries that require wood and iron for their basis; as, for instance, the manufacturing of Agricultural Implements, Railway Cars, Carriages, Wagons, etc. Kentucky offers unsurpassed advantages for the creation of industries —the widest markets with the least carriage."

ST. PAUL'S CHURCH (ROMAN CATHOLIC.)

This imposing structure, Rev. Ferdinand Brossart, Pastor, is located
on Short Street, fronting Spring, and is the only church in the city provided with a turret clock. The Catholic Church in Lexington owes its
existence to the Rev. Stephen T. Badin, a native of France, and the first
priest of his church ever ordained in this country. He escaped from Bor-
deaux during the French Revolution while the Jacobins were slaughtering
his fellow-priests, and was sent in 1794 to this city, where he labored faith-
fully for many years. Rev. G. A. M. Elder, founder of St. Joseph's College, Bardstown, and Dr. Kendrick, afterwards Archbishop of Baltimore,
were pastors of the church here. Rev. John H. Bekkers, under whose su-

pervision St. Paul's Church was completed, sleeps under its tower, which is
a most appropriate monument to his memory. The late Mrs. Abraham
Lincoln was born in the house adjoining this church, and now occupied by
Father Brossart.

ST. PETER's CHURCH (Catholic)—Rev. Jas. Kehoe, Officiating Priest—
Is located on Limestone Street, between Second and Third. This is the
oldest of the two Catholic Churches, having been erected in 1837. Adjoining it is the Nunnery and Academy of St. Catharine.

KENTUCKY ASSOCIATION RACE COURSE.

This famous race course is located at the east end of Fifth street, and
is reached by the street cars. The grounds are kept in fine order ; the
track and the grand stand are models of their kind ; no expense has been
spared to make everything as convenient and complete as lovers of the turf
could desire, and this course is now regarded as one of the handsomest in the
United States. The Kentucky Association, organized in 1826, is the oldest
racing club in this country, and stands among the very first for reputation,
popularity and success. Its meetings are held early in May and September,
and are always attended by great throngs of eager and excited people, hundreds of whom are from all parts of the country, for no where in the world is
the race horse seen under more favorable auspices than right here upon his
native blue grass, where he attains his highest development and perfection.
The region around Lexington has been called "the Breeder's Paradise," and
is already as renowned for the quality and quantity of its thoroughbreds as
was classic Thessaly of old. The Kentucky Association is itself a striking
epitome of this general character. The birthplace of "Lexington," the greatest race horse of his time, and the greatest sire that was ever foaled, can be
seen from the grand stand of the Association. Grey Eagle, Asteroid, Longfellow, Enquirer and a host of other kings of the turf were bred almost within hearing of its drum taps, and its old course has been the scene of the *debut*
and triumphs of the most noted horses that have figured in America for
years. One of the "sights" of Kentucky is Lexington during race week,
with its overflowing hotels, acres of vehicles, crowds of gesticulating sports-
men, noisy and excited negro hackmen, and the hurrahing multitude and
flying horses at the race course. The tourist can see and hear more "hoss"
then in one day than he ever heard before in all the days of his life. Pres-
dent of the Association, J. F. Robinson ; Secretary, J. B. Ferguson.

THE KENTUCKY ASSOCIATION RACE COURSE.

DISTILLERIES.

Our mammoth distilleries, which make so large a proportion of the finest whiskies of commerce, and which are located in the heart of the district, celebrated the wide world over for its production of "Old Bourbon," constitute another prominent feature of the suburbs. The visitors to these establishments will be impressed by their great capacity and enormous consumption of grain, can see for himself the curious process of whisky manufacture, and may realize to some extent the magnitude of the interest in Kentucky, in which so many millions are invested, and from which the Government derives such a vast amount of revenue. The distilleries are all located on leading turnpikes, and the majority of them are so near the city that they can be reached in a ten minutes drive.

The Henry Clay Distillery, J. E. Pepper & Co., proprietors, is on the old Frankfort pike, only a half mile from the city limits.

The Ashland Distillery, Wm. Tarr & Co , proprietors, is on the same road, and about eighty yards from the Louisville, Cincinnati & Lexington railroad.

D. A. Aikens' Distillery is near the city limits, on the line of the Big Sandy railroad.

Stoll, Clay & Co.'s Distillery, at Sandersville, is two and a half miles out, and on the line of the Cincinnati Southern railway.

Woodland Distillery, Headly & Peck, proprietors, is a mile and a half out, on the Harrodsburg pike.

Silver Spring Distillery, N Harris, proprietor, is six miles out, on the Leesburg road.

H. D. Owings' Distillery is on the Russell pike, three and a half miles from the city.

LEXINGTON'S GREAT LUMBER ADVANTAGES

Ought to make her the seat of the most extensive manufactories of furniture, wagons, agricultural implements, and like articles in this country, for she is the cheapest market in it for that kind of material. The best quality of clear, butt-cut white oak needed for manufacturing purposes can be had here at $20 per thousand. It costs about double that price in Boston. Ash, such as is used in carriage making and farm machines, at like figures. Building oak $14 per thousand. Upper grades of poplar away below what is paid at Eastern points. Furniture, and particularly poplar furniture, can be made here cheaper than at any other place in the United States. Lexington offers immense advantages over Eastern and Northern cities in this line in the price of the raw material, and fuel, and in rents and freight rates, and as a distributing point for a vast stretch of Southern country can not be excelled. The attention of capitalists and manufacturers is especially called to these, significant facts which will well repay investigation.

JOHNS.

PHOTO.

MADISON HOUSE.

The student home of Jefferson Davis;

This old building, which stands on the southwest corner of High and Limestone, is an object of especial interest, from the fact that it was the home of Hon. Jefferson Davis while he was a student at Transylvania University about sixty years ago. The now aged and famous chieftain was then a slender, fair-haired youth, noted only for his unassuming manners and studious habits. The house, which at that time was considered quite handsome, was then the private residence of the postmaster, Joseph Ficklin, with whom the future President of the Confederate States lived during his college days. It is now, and has been for many years, a boarding house.

INTERNAL REVENUE.

This collection district—the Seventh—of which Lexington is the headquarters, augmented by the late consolidation is now not only the largest in this State, but is one of the most important in the whole country. Its collections for the fiscal year ending June 30th, 1883, amounted to $1,973,863.32. This was before the consolidation. The collections hereafter will be immense. A. M. Swope, Collector. Office, 2d story of Fayette National Bank building, corner Main and Upper.

MANUFACTORIES.

Experience has plainly demonstrated that interior towns must look to something else than mercantile business to give them growth and prosperity. It is by manufacturing enterprises that such towns succeed, and Lexington realizes the fact. She wants pushing, experienced, enterprising manufacturers, regardless of where they come from or to what school of politics they belong, if they are willing to help us build up this town. We want factories to work up our raw material, and to turn out watches, hats, brooms, crackers, soap, candles, glue, cigars, &c ; tanneries, laundries, silver-plating shops, brick-yards, and a host of other industries   Persons seeking a location for their skill and capital will do well to examine the advantages of Lexington.

WOODBURN.

For lovers of fine stock to come to Lexington and not visit its almost suburban attraction—Woodburn—is equal to seeing Hamlet with Hamlet left out, for Woodburn is the most noted and extensive breeding establishment of its kind in this country. This grand place, which comprises about three thousand acres, is adjacent to Spring Station on the Lexington and Louisville railroad, only a few minutes ride from this city, and is the home of Mr. A. J. Alexander. It was here that old Lexington, the greatest race horse of his time, passed his days, and is the present home of King Alfonso (sire of Foxhall) ; Imp. Glen Athol, Falsetto, Pat Malloy, Asteroid, and more than a hundred other thoroughbreds. Harold, the sire of Maud S , Miss Russell, dam of Maud S., and Lord Russell, the full brother, and Belmont, sire of Wedgewood, represents the trotting department of about one hundred and twenty-five head. The Duke and Duchess of Airdrie, names familiar to the Shorthorn world, stand at the head of a herd of sixty fine cattle. Add to these attractions, the Southdown sheep and Shetland ponies, and one has a faint idea of the beauty that animates the Blue Grass pastures of Woodburn. The annual sales at Woodburn draw strangers from all parts of the United States.

HAROLD (sire of Maud S., 2:10½.)

SECRET AND BENEVOLENT ORDERS.

MASONIC.

LEXINGTON LODGE, No. 1, meets at Masonic Hall, corner of Walnut and Short, first and third Fridays of each month.

DAVIESS LODGE, No. 22, meets at Masonic Hall.

DEVOTION LODGE, No. 160, meets at Odd Fellows' Hall first and third Tuesdays in each month.

GOOD SAMARITAN LODGE, No. 174, meets first and third Thursdays in each month.

LEXINGTON R. A. CHAPTER, No. 1, meets at Masonic Hall second Thursday in each month.

WEBB COMMANDERY, No. 2, stated conclave at Masonic Hall second Friday in each month.

ODD FELLOWS.

FRIENDSHIP LODGE, No. 5 (founded May 6, 1837), meets every Friday in the Odd Fellows' Temple, on Main, near Limestone.

COVENANT LODGE, No. 22, meets at Odd Fellows' Temple every Saturday.

MERRICK LODGE, No. 31, meets at Odd Fellows' Temple every Monday.

BETHESDA ENCAMPMENT, No. 15, meets at Odd Fellows' Temple first and third Tuesdays in each month.

LEXINGTON DEGREE LODGE, No. 3, meets at Odd Fellows' Temple second and Fourth Wednesdays in each month.

KNIGHTS OF HONOR.

UNA LODGE, No. 518, at Odd Fellows' Temple second and fourth Thursday nights in every month.

HOME LODGE, at Odd Fellows' Temple every Thursday night.

KNIGHTS OF PYTHIAS.

PHANTOM LODGE, No. 15, Odd Fellows' Temple every Wednesday night.

ROYAL TEMPLARS OF TEMPERANCE.

HOPE COUNCIL, No. 1, Odd Fellows' Temple first and third Tuesdays in each month.

KNIGHTS OF THE GOLDEN RULE.

Meet at Odd Fellows' Temple first and third Thursday nights in each month.

ANCIENT ORDER UNITED WORKMEN.

FAYETTE LODGE, No. 4, meets over Miller & Gough's second and fourth Thursday nights in each month.

MUTUAL LODGE, No. 11, meets over Miller & Gough's first Monday night in each month.

INDRPENDENT ORDER B'NAI-B'RITH.

LEXINGTON LODGE, No. 289, meets at Odd Fellows' Temple first and fourth Sundays in each month.

INDEPENDENT ORDER OF FORRESTERS.

COURT HOBAH, No. 8, meets at Odd Fellows' Temple first Friday of each month.

ASHLAND LODGE OF GOOD TEMPLARS.

Meets at Odd Fellows' Lodge every Saturday night.

GERMAN BENEVOLENT SOCIETY.

Meets at Kruse & Hartman's Hall, on Main street, first Sunday in every month.

ASHLAND HOUSE.

Not the least of Lexington's attractions to strangers are her well managed hotels, and the Ashland House is one of them. It is centrally located on Short street, only a half a square from the post-office and banks. The proprietors, H. E. Boswell & Son, have made a fine reputation by keeping up a good table, and proving in other ways that they know how to "keep a hotel."

HISTORIC POINTS.

HENRY CLAY was married (1799) in the house on the corner of Mill and Second, now occupied by Mrs. Ann Ryland.

JOE H. DAVIESS, the great prosecutor of Burr, lived in the house on Main, opposite the Christian Church, and now occupied by Mr. Montague.

GENERAL JAMES WILKINSON lived, about 1785, on the corner of Main street and the alley adjoining the Colored Baptist Church.

"MAD" ANTHONY WAYNE inspected recruits for the Indian campaign of 1794 back of the Carty residence on Broadway.

LAFAYETTE was received by the Masons in 1825 at their hall, which then stood near the corner of Main and Broadway, on the site of the building now occupied by Curry, Howard & Murray.

JOHN BRADFORD published the first Kentucky newspaper, "The Kentucke Gazette," in 1787, on Maguire's corner, Main and Broadway. He lived and died in the Ryland residence, corner of Mill and second.

GEN. JOHN H. MORGAN'S old home is on the corner of Mill and Second, where his mother still resides.

COLONEL ROBERT PATTERSON, the founder of Lexington, and one of the founders of Cincinnati, lived on the site of the Hayes residence, corner of Hill and Lower.

HUMPHREY MARSHALL, the able Federalist partisan, and author of Marshall's History of Kentucky, died in the residence at the head of Sixth street.

McKINNEY'S SCHOOLHOUSE, where in 1783 occurred the celebrated fight with the wildcat, was on Cheapside, between the present Gazette office and the bank building.

EDWARD WEST, who, it is claimed, invented the first steamboat, launched his model in 1793 on Town Fork, at the L. C. and L. freight depot, where the water had been dammed up for the purpose.

JOEL T. HART, a Kentuckian, and one of the greatest of American sculptors, had his studio in the rear of the Bradley residence, on Second street.

RICHARD H. MENIFEE lived at the Huston place, on the Harrodsburg turnpike, where Gen. John C. Breckinridge also lived at one time.

MATT H. JOUETT, the greatest painter Kentucky has yet produced, had his studio in a building which stood where the front yard of the Northern Bank building now is. He was visited there by Gen. Andrew Jackson, President Monroe and Lafayette.

JESSE BLEDSOE lived at the Barnes place, head of Walnut street.

Continued on page 56.]

ENTRANCE TO LEXINGTON CEMETERY.

At the West end of Main Street, just beyond the crossing of the Kentucky Central Railroad, is the Lexington cemetery, one of the loveliest places of its size and kind in this country, and no stranger should leave the city without paying it a visit. Nature, art and associations have all combined to make it attractive, and it is adorned with many handsome monuments, statues and beautiful memorials that are well worth inspection. Here rests "the Sage of Ashland;" John Morgan, the brilliant partisan leader of the South; General John C. Breckinridge, Chief Justice Robertson, Colonel Morrison, General Combs, Francis K. Hunt, Gen. Gordon Granger, Hugh McKee, and many others distinguished in the history of Kentucky and the nation. Here also are the honored graves of a large number of Federal and Confederate soldiers who "sleep their last sleep, and have fought their last battle."

JAMES BROWN's residence was on the corner of Short and Mill—Wolverton building.

COL. JAMES MORRISON, founder of Morrison College, lived in the building, corner of Short and Upper, now occupied by Third National Bank. He died in Washington, D. C , April 23, 1823. and is buried in the Lexington cemetery.

THOMAS F. MARSHALL, the brilliant orator, occupied the present law office of Judge R. A. Buckner on Jordan's Row, near the corner of Short

MRS. RHODA VAUGHN, daughter of Capt. Holder, and the first white woman born in Kentucky, is buried in the Episcopal cemetery, on Third Street, west of Dewees.

DR. BEN DUDLEY, the distinguished surgeon, had his office for many years in the residence on the corner of Mill and Church, now occupied by E. D. Sayre.

GEORGE NICHOLAS, one of the ablest of early Kentucky statesmen, lived on the site of the Sayre Institute.

CASSIUS M. CLAY conducted "The True American" (which was suppressed in 1845) in the rear of Smith's drug store, corner of Mill and Main.

ROBERT WICKLIFFE lived at the Preston place, corner of Second and Jefferson.

GEORGE ROBERTSON's residence was on the corner of Mill and High.

AUNT NANCY LEE (colored), born Aug. 4, 1775, the only living person who saw Lexington when it was a frontier settlement, lives on Short. between Limestone and Walnut.

FAYETTE NATIONAL BANK AND HIGGINS BLOCK.

These handsome buildings, which speak so well for the business enterprise of the city, are located on Main and Upper streets. The Fayette National, Squire Bassett, President, and R. S. Bullock, Cashier, stands directly on the corner of the two streets, and occupies the site of the old Brent Tavern, noted as the place where Aaron Burr and his fellow-conspirators held a secret meeting in the interest of their grand scheme to found a new empire.

The engraving of this block was made from a photograph by Johns, whose beautifully executed pictures fully demonstrate Lexington's facilities for turning out first-class photographic work.

FAYETTE NATIONAL BANK AND HIGGINS BLOCK.

LEXINGTON MANUFACTORIES.

AWNINGS—T. A. Hornsey, 24 West Short.

BASKETS—George Koonz, Broadway, near Main.

BEE HIVES—Williamson & Bro., 122 West Main.

BREAD—J. W. Lell, 19 North Broadway; T. McNamara, 190 South Broadway; M. Dunleavy, 66 Manchester; P. Dockery, 140 West Short.

BLANK BOOKS—Transylvania Printing Company, 52 East Main; E. B. Smith, 16½ West Main.

BOTTLING WORKS—M. Benckart, 39 East Third.

BRICKS—G. D. Wilgus, 77 North Limestone.

CANDY—J. W. Lell, 19 North Broadway.

CARRIAGES—J. V. Upington & Bro., 102 East Short; Baker & Bro., 12 North Limestone; C. Gormley, 28 North Limestone; H. Weiman, 63 West Main ; Ely & Bro., 178 East Main.

CIGARS—J. Robinson, West Main; J. R. Reinberger, West Main; M. Feller, 12 South Mill.

COPPER WORKS—R. D. Williams, 58 West Short.

COOPER SHOPS—Blue Grass Cooper Shops, 199 East High; E. & J. Dowling, 246 West Main; A. J. Oots, 239 West Main.

GAS FACTORY—West Main, between Spring and Lower.

GRASS SEED CLEANERS—I. B. Sandusky & Co., West Short; Carroll & Son, West Main.

HEMP (Dressed) — W. Frazer & Co., 130 North Broadway ; J. F Scott & Bro., 58 West Third; Loughridge & Nelson, Seventh, between Limestone and Upper : R. C. Morgan & Co., Fourth street ; Graves & McClelland, corner Broadway and Vine ; J. Yellman, 243 West Third.

HORSE BOOTS—J. R. Shedd, 77 East Main.

ICE FACTORY—West Main, facing Jefferson.

MALT HOUSES—Luigart & Harting, North Limestone, city limits. Wolf & Farris, North Upper, between Fifth and Sixth.

MACHINE SHOPS—S. Simcox, 75 West Vine; R. D. Williams, 60 West Short.

MARBLE WORKS—Wm. Adams & Sons, 42 North Broadway; M. Pruden & Co., 44 West Main.

PLANING MILLS—E. R. Spotswood & Son, 180 East Main; F. Bush & Son, Short street ; Williamson & Bro., 122 West Main.

PAINT (Roof)—J. H. Hallowell, 115 West Vine.

SADDLES AND HARNESS—Thompson & Boyd, 53 East Main; Barkley & Pilkington, 63 East Main; McCabe & Co., 5 South Mill; C. Hottes, 10

North Limestone; T. O'Brien, 7 North Limestone; A. Davis, 17 North Limestone; J. M. Hayes, 53 East Short; J. Faig, 16 West Short.

SAW MILL—B. Fitts, Manchester.

SCALE WORKS—C. Wailey, 141 East Short.

SOAP FACTORY—Allen & Sheely, 18 West Vine.

TINWARE—M. G. Thompson, 14 South Upper; W. J. Houlihan & Bro., 26 West Main; L. P. Milward, 3 West Main; H. A. White, 23 West Short; Alex Miller, 42 West Main; Crosthwait & Son, 20 West Short.

TWINE FACTORIES—Yellman & Bro., Georgetown, near Fourth; Lexington Hemp Mills, West Main, near railroad crossing.

WAGON MAKERS—J. Rumsey, 124 East Short; W. H. Newberry, 46 North Limestone; P. H. Feeny, 57 West Main; H. Weitzel, 64 West Short; Willis Bell, 97 West Short.

WOOLEN MILLS—Loud & Bro., cor. Water and Ayres; Bosworth & Bro., Frankfort pike, near city limits.

FLOUR MILLS—Hayman & Co., 2 and 4 Vine; W. Armstrong, 115 East Short; Nottnagle & Bro., 66 Walnut; J. S. Hutsell, 127 East Third.

IMP. KING BAN.

THE PHŒNIX HOTEL.

This famous hostelrie is located on the corner of Main and Limestone streets, and though entirely new and modern in all its appointments, is in one sense the oldest hotel in the whole Western country, for it has with various changes, continued to exist ever since the year 1800. Early in this century its ancient predecessor was destroyed by fire, but only to rise quickly from its ashes in an improved form, displaying upon its front a quaint·representation of the fabled Phœnix. whose name it has continued to bear from that day to this.   It was here that Aaron Burr lodged in the fall of 1806, while engaged in his daring conspiracy to make himself the head of a new empire, and was here met and welcomed by Harman Blannerhassett, the cultured, but unfortunate, Irishman he had so completely fascinated. Here, as far back as Jefferson's administration, Democrats and Federalists, in knee-buckled breeches, ruffled shirts and dangling cues, talked red-hot politics, and here one August day in 1812 a dense throng of ladies, in long-waisted dresses and with powdered hair, towering aloft on cushions, waved farewell to the gallant Kentucky volunteers who marched so proudly past the old tavern on their way to the fatal field of Raisin.   It was the scene of a sumptuous dinner to Lafayette, and later was the stopping place of the wily Mexican chieftain, General Santa Anna.   During the late war, while Lexington was held by the Confederates, it was the headquarters of Generals Bragg and Kirby Smith, and before the struggle ended sheltered General Grant.   President Arthur has also been its guest.   It has flourished since the time it was a low-roofed. weather-boarded old inn, with a stile block, creaking sign board, and crowd of bowing and merry-hearted slaves. It has passed through the days of stage coaches, big log fires and tallow candles, and now new, commodious and conducted in number one style by a natural-born hotel keeper, Mr. C. F. Simonds, it is up with the times of steam and the electric light.   In addition to the attractions of its table and other first-class appointments, it has a telegraph office and splendid restaurant under its roof, is the seat of the Lexington Club, and extends to the depot of the Cheseapeake and Ohio and Kentucky Central Railroads, so that passengers and baggage are landed right at its doors.

FAYETTE, the county of which Lexington is the seat of justice, is bounded on the north by Scott county, on the south by Madison and Jessamine, on the east by Bourbon, and on the west by Woodford, It is twenty-five miles from north to south, mean breadth eleven miles. and contains 275 square miles, or 176,000 acres.

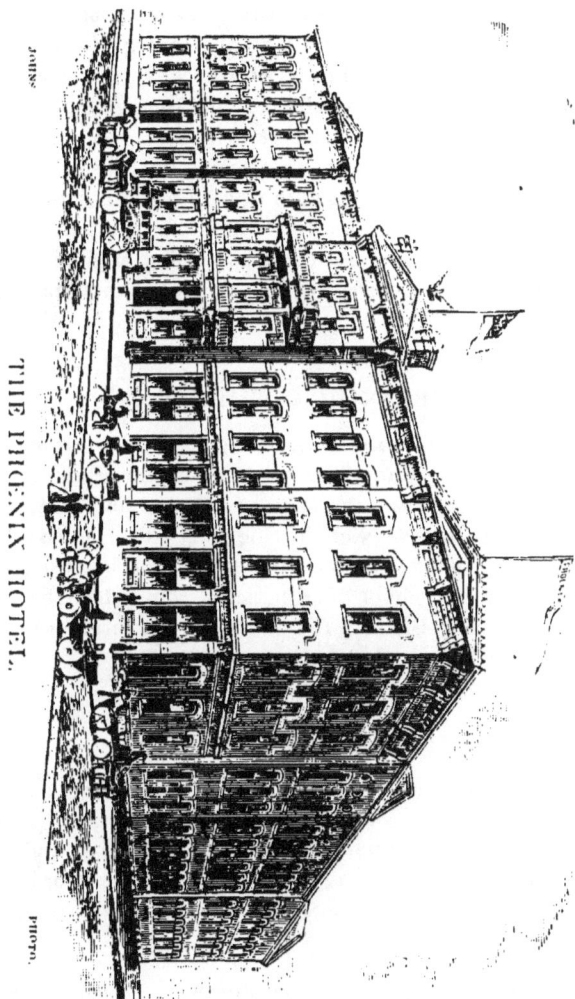

THE PHŒNIX HOTEL.

"DIXIANA."

"Dixiana." the beautiful stud farm of the noted turfman, Major B. G
Thomas, and one of the suburban attractions of Lexington, is situated on
the Russell Road, near Russell Cave, six miles north of the city, contains
two hundred and fifty acres of rich blue grass, watered by North Elkhorn
creek, and is devoted by its proprietor exclusively to breeding and training
race horses. To think of "Dixiana" is to think of Herzog, Himyar, Fellowcraft, King Ban, Lelaps, and other thoroughbreds who have made themselves famous. A handsome sign-board over the front gate of "Dixiana"
is one of the most unique and expressive features of the place. It says :
"Nothing except a good race horse wanted. Agents for the sale of books,
patent medicines, sewing machines, wheat fans, corn planters, and *especially*
lightning rods, not admitted. Visitors who will come to my house·are always welcome." If a tourist, anxious to see something original, can't find
it in that sign-board, his last chance will be to visit the mountains of the
moon.

MAMBRINO PATCHEN.

This great trotting stallion, so well known to horsemen throughout the
country, and own brother to Lady Thorne, who sold for $33,000, will be
found by visitors at Forrest Park, the farm of the veteran breeder, Dr. L.
Herr, a mile from the city, on the Nicholasville pike. This noted establishment, with its hundred head of fast stock, mile track, and extensive stables,
is the pioneer trotting horse school of Kentucky, from which fleet-footed
graduates have gone to every State in the Union. Few turfmen who come
to Lexington fail to visit Forrest Park.

HORSEMEN'S HEADQUARTERS.

This large and handsome stable, owned and conducted by Messrs.
B. J. Treacy and G. D. Wilson, is located on Main street, near the Phœnix
Hotel, and is one of the most complete establishments of its kind in this
country. Nothing strikes an observing visitor to Lexington more than the
number and immensity of the "horse hotels" that abound in the city.

THE LIBERTY POLE (1788). conspicuous during the Alien and Sedition
excitement of John Adams's administration. was located on the corner of
Main and Cheapside.

"DIVANA."

[Stud Farm of Maj. B. G. Thomas.

THE PEPPER DISTILLERY.

This extensive establishment, which marks the interesting spot where Lexington was so romantically named in 1775 (see "Wilderness Spring),") is the property of James E. Pepper & Company, and is located on the old Frankfort pike, half a mile from the city limits. It is a most complete concern, being provided with all the modern appliances, has a floor space in distillery and warehouse of 63,000 square feet; consumes an average of 550 bushels of grain per day, and produces annually 1,100 barrels of the noted Henry Clay and "Pepper" whiskies, made after the genuine, old-fashioned, hand made sour-mash process—a process which the tourist will have no chance to observe anywhere outside the State of Kentucky, from the simple fact that no hand made sour-mash whisky is manufactured anywhere else. The distillery is under the personal supervision of Mr. James E. Pepper, whose grandfather is said to have built the first distillery erected in the then wilderness district of Kentucky. The fine internal arrangements of this establishment; its cleaning and grinding apparatus; its numerous tubs of 'mash;" the "beer;" the process of distillation; the stills, and the barreling and stamping of the whisky itself, furnishes a curious sight to visitors to the greatest "Bourbon" region of the world.

WOODLAND PARK.

This beautiful place, the principal pleasure resort of Lexington, is located on east Main street, just within the city limits, and is reached by the street cars, which carry visitors directly to its gates. The place originally belonged to Mr. Irwin, a son-in-law of Henry Clay, and owes its name to the fact that it embraced one of the most exquisitely beautiful stretches of woodland to be seen in the whole Blue Grass Region. The park was the seat of the State Agricultural College when it was established in connection with Kentucky University, and several of the brick residences about it were erected for the use of professors in that institution. Woodland Park is provided with a commodious park house, where balls and other entertainments are given, an amphitheatre, base ball grounds, bicycle track, music hall, swings, &c. Usual admission fee, five cents. No intoxicating liquors allowed on the grounds. Mr. J. H. Hopson is the lessee.

The engraving of the Park (see illustration) was made from a fine photograph by Mullen, the well-known artist, whose first-class productions have done so much to secure for Lexington her extended reputation in this line of art.

THE PEPPER DISTILLERY.

JOHNS   PHOTO.

CHRIST CHURCH (EPISCOPAL).

CHRIST CHURCH, Rev. Thos. A. Tidball, Rector, located on the corner of Church and Market streets, is the only church edifice of pure Gothic architecture in the city, and is noted for the elegance and spaciousness of its interior, a beautiful memorial window, the gift of Mrs. E. B. Woodward, being one of its adornments. Christ Church, which has always occupied the same site, was organized in 1796 by Rev. James Moore, the first minister of the Episcopal Church of the United States to settle permanently in Kentucky, and the first President of Transylvania University. His memorial tablet can be seen in the inner front wall of the edifice. Rev. B. B. Smith, now the Presiding Bishop of the Episcopal Church of the United States, was rector of Christ Church for many years, as was also Rev E. F. Berkley, who preached Mr. Clay's funeral sermon, and Dr. Shipman, present pastor of Christ Church, New York City. The funeral services of General John H. Morgan were conducted in this building.

ST. ANN'S CHURCH, EPISCOPAL (Colored)—Rev. J. B. McConnell, Pastor—Is on Fourth street, between Upper and Limestone.

WOODLAND PARK. (See page 64.)

MULLEN

WEISBRODT CIN O

PHOT

LEXINGTON'S MANUFACTURING ADVANTAGES.

The remarkable advantages which this city offers for the establishment of manufactories are attracting deserved attention, and are destined to make her one of the important industrial points of the Ohio valley. She can easily feed an army of artisans and mechanics, for she is the food depot of the land of abundance, the Blue Grass Region of Kentucky, which produces more of the necessaries and luxuries of life than any other equal section of country in the world. She enjoys a climate especially favorable to continuous mechanical labor and its various productions, for it is temperate, signally exempt from extremes, storms and epidemics, and is pre-eminent for healthfulness, as reference to national statistics will show. She has an inexhaustible supply of water that can be reached at any point by boring to a moderate depth. She has more educational institutions, including colleges, universities and five public schools, than any city of the same size in America, and eighteen churches flourish under the auspices of the leading religious bodies of the country. She has street railways, gas, telephones, good markets, free mail delivery, and all other public conveniences necessary to an industrial population, as these pages plainly indicate. She proposes to exempt manufacturers, and especially those employing skilled labor, from taxation for a term of years. She is located in the very midst of the most productive hemp and tobacco section of this country, with a character of labor especially adapted to their manufacture—a region which furnishes a large amount of wool and which yields the wheat most desired for the flour trade of South America. She has an industrial element among her white population, both male and female, of superior character and intelligence, anxious for mechanical employment, particularly in establishments in which they may be trained and become useful at skilled labor. She is a railroad center. The Chesapeake and Ohio, the Cincinnati Southern, Louisville and Nashville, Kentucky Central, Lexington and Maysville, and Kentucky Union railways afford her commercial intercourse in every direction, shipping facilities unsurpassed by any other city in the State, and cheaper freights east and South than either Cincinnati or Louisville. She has inexhaustib'e supplies of cheap raw materials for manufacturing almost at her doors, for her railroads have opened up to her the wonderful resources of the neighboring counties of Eastern Kentucky. From thence they bring her low-priced coal from a field whose area exceeds that of the coal field of England, and whose seams are from three to eight feet in thickness. Many of the coals equal the best Pittsburg, and one of them, the cannel, took the premium at the Centennial Exposition at Philadelphia as the finest in the world. The character of the immense iron resources of this region is displayed in the celebrated Red River car wheel iron found on the Kentucky Union Railroad, only forty-five miles from Lexington. Nowhere in this country can iron be produced cheaper, and no ores of equal richness are to be found so convenient to pure, cheap coals. The timber of this region is of the greatest extent and variety, is of inestimable value, and includes the finest virgin hard wood known in America. Old forest walnut that can not be surpassed, black birch, hickory, white oak, red maple, yellow poplar, chestnut, elms, lindens, locust and buckeyes abound. Salt, gypsum, clays for pottery and fire brick, building stone, hydraulic limestone and other valuable substances are abundant.

From this brief summary it is evident that Lexington offers superior advantages for the manufacture of railroad materials, agricultural implements of every description, woodenware, furniture, tobacco, hempen materials, leather and leather goods, pottery, terra cotta articles, wagons, fine vehicles, woolen goods, watches, delicate machinery and artistic productions, and for the location of iron works, machine shops, mills, factories and industrial establishments of many kinds.

THE STATE COLLEGE

Or more correctly speaking, "the Agricultural and Mechanical College of Kentucky," is finely situated at the south end of Limestone street, in the midst of the noted old Maxwell Spring grounds of fifty acres, once the property of John Maxwell, a companion of Boone, and one of the founders of Lexington. The handsome and imposing buildings are entirely new, having just been completed last year, and are heated by steam and supplied with all the modern conveniences. The view from the central tower is exceedingly fine. One of the attractions of the institution is a splendid archæological collection, presented by the Government. The Agricultural and Mechanical College was organized in 1866, is entirely unsectarian, is under the exclusive control of the State, and affords a large number of students of limited means all the advantages of an able faculty free of tuition. A normal department and military training are prominent features of the institution. The attendance is large, and if its late rapid increase is continued will soon amount to six hundred or seven hundred students. Professor James K. Paterson, widely known as an educator, is the accomplished President of the college, and he is assisted by a full corps of professors distinguished for their learning. The State College, ably conducted and splendidly equipped, affords every facility for a thorough education, and is the pride of Lexington, noted as she is for the number and high character of her educational advantages.

NOTED LOCALITIES.

AARON BURR and alleged conspirators met in 1806 in a building replaced by the Fayette National Bank, on the corner of Main and Upper.

HORACE HOLLY, the brilliant President of Transylvania University, had a residence in 1818 adjoining the old college building, which then stood in Gratz Park.

THE FIRST STONE SILL of the Western railroad, afterwards known as the "Lexington and Frankfort," was laid at the corner of Mill and Water, Oct. 21, 1831.

THE FIRST CHURCH established in Lexington was "Mt. Zion," Presbyterian (1784). and stood on the site of City School No. 1, corner of Short and Walnut.

FORT CLAY, erected by Gen. Gilmore of the Federal army, was near the Versailles turnpike, overlooking the Cincinnati Southern Railroad. The remains of an earth-work can still be seen at the Association Course.

JOHN POPE lived at the Woolfolk place, corner of Hill and Rose, where William T. Barry subsequently lived.

LIVE STOCK ESTABLISHMENTS.

Many establishments devoted to the breeding and training of fine stock are located near the city, a number of which rank among the most extensive and successful of their kind in America, and are of themselves worth a visit to Lexington to see. They are always open to strangers, who never fail to receive a hearty Kentucky welcome and every facility to see the sights. See lists on pages 78 and 80.

THE CHAMBER OF COMMERCE.

This important institution, organized to promote the commercial and industrial interests of Lexington, is located in Lell's Hall, on Short street, near the post office.   It represents the capital, the public spirit, and the business intelligence of the city, gives them their freest and most influential expression, and unites and concentrates the strength of the business men, thus making their efforts in behalf of the trade and advancement of the city tenfold more effective.   The Chamber is deeply interested in building up manufactories in Lexington, for which industries the city affords unusual advantages, and all laudable enterprises of this character receive the prompt and

earnest attention of this body. Its members are wide-awake, and extend a
hearty invitation to capitalists, manufacturers, mechanics and business men
generally, to locate among them and share the blessings of this highly favored
region. The Chamber of Commerce has rejuvenated Lexington. Its officers are : President, J. H. Davidson ; Vice Presidents, W. B. Emmal and
W. S. McChesney; Board of Directors, Alexander Pearson, M. Kaufman,
W. C. P. Breckinridge, J. W. Lell, R. P. Stoll, E. C. Piatt, G. W. Ranck ;
Secretary, R. J. O'Mahoney

Lell's Hall, the strikingly handsome building in which the sessions of the
Chamber of Commerce are held, was lately erected by J. W. Lell, one of the
most enterprising and public spirited citizens of Lexington.

CHRISTIAN CHURCHES.

THE MAIN STREET CHRISTIAN CHURCH — Elder W. F. Cowden,
Pastor — is located on Main Street, only a few steps east of the Phœnix Hotel, and is noteworthy, not only for accommodating the largest
congregation in the city, but as the building in which occurred in 1843 the
debate between Bishop Alexander Campbell and Rev. N. L. Rice, with
Henry Clay as one of the Moderators. The history of the Church of Christ
in Lexington begins with the year 1825, when one little religious, body under
the leadership of the able and scholarly Barton W. Stone, and another
holding the then newly advanced views of the distinguished Alexander
Campbell, began to attract public attention. The two churches subsequently uniting, formed the present Christian Church of Lexington. Memories
of the powerful and original Lard, of the poetically eloquent Dr. Pinkerton,
of the devoted and accomplished President Milligan of Kentucky University,
and of others whose voices are now silent, cluster about the Main Street
Church.

THE BROADWAY CHRISTIAN CHURCH-Eld. J. S. Shouse, Pastor--stands
on the corner of Broadway and Second Streets. This church was organized
as an independent body in 1871, with Elder J. W. McGarvey as pastor.
It is located in one of the best quarters of the city, and has lately been very
handsomely improved.

THE CONSTITUTION STREET CHRISTIAN CHURCH (Colored)—Elder
H. M. Ayres, Pastor—South side of Constitution Street, between Limestone
and Walnut. This is the most tasteful church edifice owned by the colored
people of the city.

JOHNe   PHOTO.

MAIN STREET CHRISTIAN CHURCH.

MAMBRINO PATCHEN. (*See page 62.*)

MULLEN   PHOTO,

SAYRE FEMALE INSTITUTE.

A view of the extensive buildings, park-like grounds and complete appointments of this noted school, which is located on Limestone street, facing
Second, will give the tourist some idea of the educational advantages which
have made Lexington so widely known as a seat of learning. Prominent
among the scientific apparatus of this institution can be seen one of those
wonderful instruments, the Planetarium, invented in Lexington by Thomas
Barlow, perfected after ten years study and labor, and awarded a medal of
the first class at the Paris Exposition. Another attractive feature to visitors
is the large gymnasium, devoted to the physical training of the pupils, and
provided with a bowling alley and the best modern appliances for exercise
and recreation. The Sayre Institute, which was established through the
munificence of that liberal patron of learning, the late David A. Sayre, of
this city, now has the benefit of the fostering care of his nephew, Mr. E. D.
Sayre, chairman of the Board of Trustees. The patronage of the school is
very large, and is most justly deserved. At the head of its full board of instructors is Major H. B. McClellan, principal, through whose scholarly
ability and untiring energy the Institute has been brought up to its present
high state of efficiency. It is a first-class school.

ASHLAND PARK STOCK FARM.

Few horse fanciers who come to Lexington go away without catching a good glimpse of Ashland Park, the well known breeding and training farm of Mr. Barney J. Treacy. It is located about a mile from the city, on the Richmond pike; comprises four hundred acres of unbroken blue grass, a fine mile track, ample stabling, and all the conveniences needed in a large and complete establishment of its kind. Woodford Abdallah, conspicuous for the richness of his thoroughbred strains, is the present head of the Ashland Park Stud of over two hundred horses of all ages, and trotters by him and the noted Abdallah West, have gone to nearly every quarter of the globe. Ashland Park was inspected by President Arthur when he visited Lexington.

EASTERN KENTUCKY LUNATIC ASYLUM.

This immense institution, the largest of any kind in the city of Lexington, and one of the most complete of its character in the United States, is situated on the Newtown pike, with its main entrance on Fourth street. The beautifully ornamented grounds embrace three hundred acres, and the handsome and imposing brick buildings, which almost equal in capacity an ordinary village, are supplied with every modern convenience, comfort and medical and scientific arrangement calculated to benefit the large number of unfortunate inmates. Since the establishment of this great public charity more than a million dollars have been spent upon it, upwards of five thousand patients have been received and treated, and of that number nearly two thousand have been discharged as recovered. This asylum, the first of its kind founded in the West, and the second State institution for the cure of the insane in this country, was incorporated in 1816, and was established through the enlightened exertions of some of the benevolent citizens of early Lexington. The building caught a stray cannon ball during the war fired by the Federals from Fort Clay during Morgan's last raid in June, 1864. Dr. R. C. Chenault is the present able Medical Superintendent. His predecessor was the faithful official, Dr. W. O. Bullock. The institution is open to visitors every Tuesday and Thursday between the hours of two and five in the afternoon. See page 81.

The breeding and training of trotting horses is conducted on a very large scale in the country surrounding Lexington, and the size and equipment of some of the institutions devoted to the education of these animals make them objects of special attention to strangers. See page 78.

ASHLAND PARK STOCK FARM.

ASHLAND PARK STOCK FARM, NEAR LEXINGTON KY, B. J. TREACY PROP.

THOROUGHBREDS AND TROTTERS.

The following is a list of the most prominent breeding and training establishments about Lexington, their distances from the city and their most noted stallions, viz :

THOROUGHBREDS.

Dixiana, B. G. Thomas, Russell road, six miles from Lexington—Imp. King Ban, Fellowcraft, Lelaps, &c.

Bryant Station, J. A. Grinstead, Bryant Station road, six miles from Lexington.

Blue Grass Park, J. A. Grinstead, Georgetown road, ten miles from Lexington—Gilroy.

Elmendorf, D. Swigert, Maysville road, five miles from Lexington—Glenelg. Prince Charlie, &c.

McGrathiana, Milton Young, Newtown road, three miles from Lexington—Onandaga.

Ashland Stock Farm, John M. Clay, Tate's Creek road, two miles from Lexington.

Lakewood, R. W Preston, Richmond road—Strachino.

Woodburn and its thoroughbreds is noticed elsewhere.

Harper's, the home of Longfellow and Ten Broeck, is near Midway, a short ride from this city.

TROTTERS

Fairlawn, W. T. Withers, North Broadway, city limits—Almont, &c.

Forrest Park. L. Herr, Nicholasville road, one mile from Lexington—Mambrino Patchen.

Ashland. H. C. McDowell, Richmond road—Dictator.

Ashland Park, B. J. Treacy, Richmond road, one and a half miles from Lexington—Abdallah West.

Westland, R. West. Versailles road, two miles from Lexington—Blackwood and Egbert.

Inwood, A. S. Talbott, near Harrodsburg road, two and a half miles from Lexington—Alcyone.

Ash Grove, W. Simmons, Old Frankfort road, five miles from Lexington—George Wilkes.

Bryant Station. P. P. Johnston, Bryant Station road, five miles from Lexington.

Walnut Grove, R. Todhunter, Richmond road, eight miles from Lexington.

Walnut Hill, Z. E. Simmons, Richmond road, six miles from Lexington —France's Alexander.

A. Smith McCann. Russell road, two miles from Lexington—Red Wilkes.

Waveland, Joseph Bryant, Nicholasville road, four miles from Lexington—Hambrino.

N. C. Stanhope South Elkhorn road, seven miles from Lexington.

Robert Prewitt, near Athens, eight miles from Lexington- Ashland Chief.

MULLEN.   PHOTO.

CITY SCHOOL, NO 3.

This large and handsome building erected in 1881, and named for Dr. Ben W. Dudley, of Transylvania University, is located on the corner of Mill and Maxwell. It is an honor to the city, and reflects the progressive spirit of her splendid public schools. Col. J R. Graves, Principal.

MORTON SCHOOL, No. 1, located on the corner of Walnut and Short Streets, is named in honor of a public spirited citizen, William Morton, who left a legacy of $10.000 to increase its usefulness.   Prof. G. D. Hunt, Principal.

HARRISON SCHOOL, No. 2, named in honor of the venerable James O. Harrison, who greatly improved the city schools, stands on West Main Street, near Jefferson.   Prof. J. B. Skinner, Principal.

Superintendent of City Schools—John O. Hodges, Jr., Esq.

In addition to the city schools named above, there is one for Catholic pupils and four for colored children, and also a goodly number of very fine private schools.

The public schools of Lexington are in a high state of efficiency and prosperity, and constitue one of the strongest inducements to the intelligent and industrious to locate in the city.   They originated in 1834, just after a terribly destructive cholera season had left many children unprovided with means of education.

SHORT-HORN HERDS.

The aristocratic cattle of this and adjoining counties should not be neglected by the tourist.   Nothing will give him a better idea of the wonderful qualities of this limestone soil than a view of the noted herds of Short-Horns which constitute so large a part of the wealth of Central Kentucky, to say nothing of the Jerseys and the Alderneys, the Cotswold and Southdown sheep, and the fine hogs.   The regular sales of Short-Horns that take place at and near Lexington every summer attract buyers from all parts of the country, and though these sales last only a few days, from $200,000 to $300,-000 worth of high-bred animals are sold at them.   The following is a list of Short-Horn breeders and distances from Lexington, Ky.

A. L. Hamilton, Tate's Creek pike, three miles.

W. W. Hamilton, Maysville pike, two and a half miles.

J. G. Kinnaird, Winchester pike, near Chilesburg.

William Warfield, Winchester pike, two miles.

W. W. Estill, Winchester pike, four miles.

David Coleman, Newtown pike, three miles.

Isaac Vanmeter, Versailles pike, five and a half miles.

Hart Boswell, Russell road, eight miles.

W. D. Boswell, Russell road, seven miles.

R. H. Innes, Russell road, ten miles.

C. W. Innes, Russell road, ten miles.

G. H. Whitney, Russell road, eight miles.

I. P. Shelby, Richmond road. nine miles.

D. H. James, Military road. eight miles, near South Elkhorn.

EASTERN KENTUCKY LUNATIC ASYLUM. (*See page 76.*)

SCHAEFER DEL

MULLEN

PHOTO.

HORSEMEN'S HEADQUARTERS. (*See page 62.*)

BELMONT. (Sire of Wedgewood, 2:15).

WATERWORKS.

A first-class system of waterworks is about to be added to Lexington's numerous advantages.   As this book goes to press a joint committee of the City Council and Chamber of Commerce is considering the best means of accomplishing this important object.   The city will be supplied with water either from the subterranean resources mentioned on page 10 or from the Kentucky River, which is about eleven miles from Lexington, and is fed by a multitude of pure mountain streams.   In either case Lexington will be one of the best watered cities in the country.

HYGEIA HOTEL.

(Old Point Comfort, Va).

Situated on Hampton Roads, one hundred yards from Fortress Monroe, is open all the year round.   By the completion of the Chesapeake and Ohio Railroad this delightful place has become almost a suburban attraction of Lexington, and crowds from the Blue Grass Region of Kentucky constantly enjoy the boating, fishing and surf bathing, and the comforts and elegancies of the hotel.   It is both a summer retreat and a winter home. United with it and under the same management is that celebrated mountain resort

THE WHITE SULPHUR SPRINGS,

Greenbrier County, West Virginia, whose health-giving waters, magnificent scenery and extensive hotel attractions have gained for it so wide a reputation that it has been called "the Baden-Baden of America."   H. Phoebus is the proprietor and lessee of these united seaside and mountain resorts.

INDEX.